Empat

A Survival Guide For Empaths.

How To Embrace Your Gift, Deal With Covert Narcissists And Dodge Energy Vampires.

Theresa Evans

EMPATH
HEALING
A SURVIVAL GUIDE FOR EMPATHS
HOW TO EMBRACE YOUR GIFT, DEAL WITH COVERT
NARCISSISTS AND DODGE ENERGY VAMPIRES
THERESA EVANS

Table Of Contents

Introduction

By the age of 13, I was severely overweight, and I could easily eat my weight in potato chips, especially if I was upset. I was on the path for major health problems, and there was a good chance that I would have found other addictions later on in life.

I was ridiculed by my mother, and the more weight I gained, the worse it got. But the thing is, it shouldn't have been this way. The "poking fun" started when I was around six or seven. I was more easily upset than my older brother had been. A loud noise would make me jump out of my skin, and if I got in trouble, it would take me hours to calm down. My mother thought this was hilarious, I suppose, and would make fun of me for it. My brother got in on it as well. I felt horrible. I thought I was "too sensitive" and that I needed to learn to "grow up". I have no self-worth, and the only thing that made me feel better was food.

Later in life, I learned that my mother was a narcissist. She used me to make herself feel good, and she didn't care how she made me feel. She was the cause of a lot of emotional abuse. This abuse caused me to fall in love with somebody, just like her. My first significant relationship was full of the same "jokes" and abuse that my childhood had been full of. Guess what happened? I stayed with him because I thought he needed me. To be fair, he didn't do a great job at making me believe just that. During this time, I tried to lose weight, but it didn't help. When he would go off on one of his tirades of how useless I was, I would eat nearly everything in the house. Luckily, we didn't keep alcohol in the house because I'm sure I would have turned to it to numb the pain I was feeling.

But, one day, a friend, one of the few I had, told me I needed help. She said, "You don't deserve to be treated that way. You are too nice of a person." I thought she was crazy. He was exactly who I thought I deserved to be with because that's all I had been taught. She gave me a business card to a therapist who could help me, and for some reason, I decided to go. This therapist is who helped me realize why I had been subjected to all of this abuse and pain during my life. I discovered I was an empath.

True empaths don't occur very often, but those of us out there tend to be more prone to abusive relationships. I wanted to know why, and I also wanted to help people who were alike. Empaths have a fantastic gift to help others, but they must first help themselves. This is why I wrote this book.

So, I set out to figure out how empaths can heal themselves and why we are so susceptible to these horrible relationships. What I have learned is laid out before you in this book.

We will go through what it means to be an empath, first. I want you to understand that you aren't strange or "too sensitive", but instead, you are a gift that can be used to help others.

Then, we will look at the neuroscience behind empathy. There are a lot of people that don't believe empaths are real, but there is science to prove that we do exist and some reasons behind why we feel what we feel.

Next, we will go through understanding the wounds from your past. Unfortunately, for most empaths, we have had to endure some type of pain before we realize what is going on. But we can heal from it and learn to avoid it in the future.

After that, we will discuss the problem of chronic fatigue and anxiety. There are areas of an empath's life that can cause more problems, and one of those areas are unfulfilling workplaces. We'll look at how jobs, along with other things, can cause anxiety and chronic fatigue in empaths.

Then we will move into getting rid of the negativity of narcissists and energy vampires. You'll find that empaths tend to be drawn to these people because we sense that they need help. The trouble is, they don't think they do, so we won't ever be able to help them.

Next, we'll look at the addiction problems that empaths can develop. As people prone to abuse, it is common for us to turn to external things to try and numb the pain.

Then we will discuss the empathic child. We want to make sure that the next generation grows up understanding who they are and not have to endure the pain that we have had to go through. It is possible for an empath to blossom into a well-rounded young adult without having to heal from years of heartache and pain.

Then we will dive into powerful recovery methods for empaths who are deeply hurt. This can be helpful for any empath, but it is aimed towards those who have gone through years of abuse, as I had, and who desperately need to heal themselves of deep wounds.

Lastly, we will go over the best ways to help your spirit-mind connection. This will help you to learn how to use your gift to help others and to connect with your spiritual self.

This book is meant to help people like me – people who have been emotionally abused by those who want to take advantage of their good nature. You aren't the one who is damaged or wrong. Those lies you have been fed your entire life are just that, lies, and you are much better and more amazing than you think.

Chapter 1: Embracing Your Empathic Gift

If you looked up a simple definition of empathy, you would get an explanation that goes something like this; "empathy is the ability to read and understand people and resonate, or be in-tune, with others." This ability to read others can be voluntary or involuntary. For natural empaths, it is involuntary.

Empaths are hypersensitive people who have extremely high levels of compassion, understanding, and consideration towards other people. Their empathy ability creates a tuning fork effect that gives the ability to feel the emotions of the people that are around them. The majority of empaths are completely unaware of the way in which all of this works. Most just simply accept the fact that they are sensitive to people.

Most empaths don't realize that there are others out there that they share traits with. When you're an empath, you are deeply affected by other people's energy, and you have a built-in affinity for intuitively perceiving and feeling the emotions of people around you. Unconsciously, you are often influenced by the desires, moods, wishes, and thoughts of others. Being an empath isn't simply being highly sensitive, and it doesn't simply stop with emotions.

Empaths can tap into a person's spiritual urges and physical sensitivities, as well as having the ability to understand their intentions and motivations. Humans are either an empath, or they aren't. There is no in-between, and true empathy cannot be learned. Natural empaths are open to process the energy and feelings of others, which means that you can actually feel, and most of the time, take on the emotions of others. Many empaths tend to experience unexplained aches and pains, chronic fatigue, and environmental sensitivities. These experiences tend to be connected to outside influences and has very little to do with you. Basically, you get to walk around with extra accumulated karma, emotions, and energy from others.

Empaths are often quiet achievers. They don't do well when given compliments because they like to show off the achievements of others. They tend to be extremely expressive in various areas of emotional connections, and they find it easy to talk openly and frankly. When somebody is willing to listen, they will talk about their feelings.

However, empaths can also be the opposite. They can be unresponsive and sometimes even reclusive. They can even come off as completely ignorant. Some learned how to block out others, and that isn't necessarily a bad thing, at least when the empath is still learning and struggling with the emotions they are sucking in from others, along with their own.

Empaths tend to be open to feeling things that are outside of them instead of their own feelings. This is why empaths will often ignore their own needs. Empaths are most often non-violent, non-aggressive, and try to keep the peace. Spaces that are often filled with disharmony tend to make empaths feel very uncomfortable. When caught up within a confrontation, empaths will try to settle the situation as quickly as possible, if not simply avoid the situations completely. If they were to say something harsh while they are trying to defend themselves, they would end up resenting themselves for lacking self-control.

Empaths often pick up on the emotions of others and then project them back without realizing where those emotions came from. Talking about things is very important for a learning empath so that they are able to release emotions. Empaths can develop stronger degrees of understanding so that they are able to find peace in different situations.

Empaths can also be sensitive to things on television, videos, news, and movies. Violent or emotional dramas that portray shocking scenes of pain that are inflicted on animals, children, or other people can cause an empath to cry.

Empaths tend to naturally gravitate towards working with animals, nature, or people because they have a strong passion to help them. They tend to be tireless caretakers and teachers for the environment and all things in it.

They tend to be great storytellers because of their always increasing knowledge, endless imagination, and inquisitive minds. They are also often old and gentle romantics at heart. They tend to be the person to go to when you want to learn something about family history and ancestry. While they may not be obvious family historians, they will be the ones that listened to the stories of the older generation and pass them down.

They tend to have a very broad interest in music because they have various temperaments, and those that are closest to them may questions how they are able to listen to one type of music one minute and minutes later switch to something completely different. The lyrics of songs can have a strong impact on empaths as well, especially if it is relevant to what they are going through.

No one is completely sure about the true mechanics of empathy and empaths. There are many theories that try to explain these things. There are a lot of empaths who don't simply have one ability, and there are some empaths who can gather information from several different abilities that work together to create a huge psychic ability. An empath can unknowingly use psychometry to learn information by touching an object or person. Their empathy will then process the information into emotions. Beyond this, the person could have other strong psychic abilities that can help them to process the information that they have received.

Benefits And Abilities

There are many benefits to be an empath. The majority of the benefits are the abilities that empathy gives you. Now, there may be times when these abilities seem like a burden, but if you use the healing and grounding practices that you will learn later on in this book, you can minimize the negative feelings you may have.

1. Empaths are highly sensitive.

Empaths are very good listeners, naturally giving, and spiritually open. If you are looking for heart, empaths will have it. Through thick and thin, the natural nurturers of the world will be there. But their feelings are also very easily hurt. Empaths will often be told to "toughen up" or that they are "too sensitive".

2. Empaths are highly intuitive.

Empaths experience things around them through their intuition. They must learn to develop this skill so that they understand how to turn into their gut feelings about others. This will end up guiding them towards positive relationships and staying away from the negative ones.

3. Empaths have heightened senses.

Empaths are able to hear and smell things at a stronger level than others. Because of this, it can cause their nerves to get easily frayed if there are excess, smells, talking, or noises.

4. Empaths simply know.

Empaths are able to pick up on things without being told. This is a knowing that is stronger than a simple gut feeling or intuition, even though that is how most will describe their knowing.

5. Empaths can easily pick up on honesty.

When someone they care about lies to them, they know it. Most empaths will try to ignore this because it hurts them to know that a person they care about would lie to them.

Possible Challenges

"With great power comes great responsibility." – Voltaire.

This statement couldn't be more true for empaths. Empathy can bring about many challenges, but most are caused by neglecting your own needs. Let's take a look at some challenges empaths may face.

1. Empaths absorb a lot of emotions.

Empaths are more tuned in to the moods of others, whether good or bad. They are able to feel everything, and sometimes this can go to extremes. They will easily take on negativity like anger and anxiety, which can end up exhausting them. If they are surrounded by love and peace, they are able to flourish.

2. Most empaths are very introverted.

Crowds will often overwhelm empaths because their empathy is amplified. They prefer smaller groups or simple one-on-one interactions. Even when an empath tends to be more extroverted, they will still limit the time they spend at parties or in large crowds.

3. Intimate relationships are often overwhelming for empaths.

Being around a person too much can be tough for empaths, so they will sometimes try to stay away from intimate relationships. Deep down, they are worried about losing their identity. For them to really feel at ease when in a relationship, they have to redefine the normal paradigm.

4. Empaths are easy targets for energy vampires.

Their sensitivities mean they are easy marks for energy vampires. These energy suckers have the ability to do more damage than simply draining the energy of the empath. Narcissists ten to be just as dangerous and can cause the empath to feel as if they are unlovable and unworthy.

5. Empaths can sometimes give too much.

Empaths have the biggest hearts in the world, and they will try to fix the pain of everybody. It's natural to want to help people who need it and try to ease their suffering, but empaths don't know when to stop. Instead, they will assume the problems of the person and will leave themselves feeling upset and drained.

6. Empaths often suffer from digestive disorders or low back problems.

The seat of the emotions is the solar plexus chakra, and it is located in the middle of the belly. This is the main location where an empath will also feel negative emotions of others, which will end up weakening this area and can cause issues like IBS and stomach ulcers. Low back issues will often happen when an empath is ungrounded, along with many other things, and a person who doesn't realize they are an empath will nearly always be ungrounded.

7. Empaths tend to have an addictive personality.

Empaths tend to turn to things like alcohol, sex, or drugs, among other things, in order to try and block out the overload of emotions they are experiencing. This is a type of self-protection so that they are able to hide from someone or something.

8. Empaths can be easily distracted.

School, home, and work must be able to keep empaths interested; otherwise, they will end up switching off and spend their time doodling or daydreaming.

Instead of letting these challenges control you, you can learn how to control them. This can be done by working with your empathy. The first thing you can do is improve your energetic literacy. There are three stages of energetic literacy.

1. When you start out with energetic literacy, you will feel lots of random things. You may start to notice where a person's energy begins, and this is also known as their aura. You may even feel scared, but you'll learn to interpret that with time. You could also see the lights or colors.

2. In the second stage, you will start to make interpretations. This could mean that you can tell that a person's root chakra is open or closed. This is also the stage where you can tell if they are lying or telling the truth.

3. In stage three, everything is open and ready to use. You can easily read a person's feelings, and you have become a human lie detector test. You could also be able to read

a person's aura, even from pictures. This is where you are in complete control of your empathy.

Within this, you will learn how to read a person's energy signature. An energy signature is just like your regular signature, but instead of ink, it is written in energy. Energy signatures can be changed, just like a radio frequency. By turning into energies and emotions, you can tell what frequency a person is vibrating on.

The important thing is to make sure you manage your afflictions. If you are feeling down or drained, tune into yourself and figure out what you need to do. You have to make sure you make yourself feel good.

Opportunities And Needs

Being an empath opens you up to many opportunities as well as needs. You are one of the few. There are not that many empaths in the world. Sure, anybody can learn to be empathetic to others, but not everybody is empathic and literally feels the emotions that others are experiencing.

1. Empaths need to have some alone time to ground.

Since empaths are super-responders, they find it very draining to be around others, so they need to have some alone time in order to recharge. A quick little escape will keep them from reaching an emotional overload. For example, empaths like to take their own cars when going somewhere so that they are able to leave whenever they want.

2. Nature helps to replenish the empath.

Regular everyday life tends to be a lot for the empath to handle. Nature can help to restore and nourish them. It provides them with a way to release all of their burdens, and they can take refuge in the ocean, or other bodies of water, and the greenery.

3. Empaths are most often drawn to metaphysical and holistic practices.

While most empaths are drawn to healing people, they most often will stay away from being healers because they end up taking on too many emotions from the patients they work with. This is especially true if they are unaware of the fact that they are an empath. Empaths tend to be open to things that a lot of other people would view as unthinkable, and they aren't often surprised or shocked by things.

4. Empaths tend to be very creative.

Every empath has natural creativity. It is simply a part of who they are, and this can be used to help express themselves and their emotions. One great way for an empath to heal is to channel their emotions into a work of art. When you go at things in the right space of mind, then your art has the ability to touch others as well. Even if you think that you are too old to begin expressing your creativity, you'll soon realize how creativity is able to teach you about yourself.

As an empath, you need to learn how to minimize your personal reaction to the information that you receive during the day. This will come with practice, but eventually, you will learn how to distinguish which emotions are somebody else’s and not yours.

I want to end this chapter with a little exercise. This will help you learn how to control your empathic abilities. Plus, it is a simple visualization tool that you can do at any time.

1. Close your eyes and begin to picture two volume switches within your mind's eye. One of these switches is labeled "me," and the other is "everyone else."

2. Reach out and grab the volume switch labeled “me” and turn it all the way up. Then, turn the other volume switch all the way down.

3. Whenever you start feeling like you can hear the roar of others, you can do this exercise. When you first start out, you may have to do this several times during the day, but the more you do it, the less often you will need to

do it. This is a great visualization to practice when you know you are getting ready to be in a crowd, or if you start to feel overwhelmed.

That's probably one of the easier exercises you will find in this book, but it will really help you.

Chapter 2: The Neuroscience Behind Empathy

There are many different things in life that look like they are magic until we can take the time to figure out the way in which they work and understand the processes involved. Unfortunately, they are still working on this part for empaths. However, there has been some research performed in different areas of neuroscience that could help to explain empaths.

Now, there is a bit of a problem when it comes to science fully believing in empaths. We know we're real. We know how we feel. But science has yet to fully find and explanation, and until then, they will continue to argue that empaths aren't real. Sometimes you just have to simply believe things exist. But I'm not here to get into that. We are actually going to go over some scientific studies that could explain empaths, even if their findings are indirect.

Mirror Neuron System

The first scientific study on empaths is the mirror neuron system. Mirror neurons are thought to be a neurophysiological mechanism that plays a part in the way we understand the actions of other people and learn to imitate them. The studies about these were first done in regard to the context of motor skills. They discovered that they were activated when a monkey watched a person do a certain action. This helped the scientists to form a hypothesis that watching a person do something would trigger a response inside of another person that helps them to mimic and imitate the things they saw. The act of seeing somebody else experience something activates various neurons in the brain even when we aren't actually performing the action.

Marco Iacoboni found that mirror neurons could have a physiological basis for morality and empathy since they play a part in how we interpret and perceive the experiences of other people around us. In the simplest explanation possible, these neurons are triggered by observing a physical gesture in a different person, which will cause the same neuron to fire in the observer. The amazing thing about this is that it is consistently happening even when a person watching doesn't move. It works as just an internal representation of something, and not an actual physical imitation.

Let's take this as an example when you are watching a football game, these neurons are triggered when the receiver catches the pass, and these same neurons are fired in the audience. This also happens when you see a person experience some type of pain or if you were to see a person with a facial expression of worry or anger. The brain has the ability to interpret the meaning of these different situations by internally experiencing them through it owns mirror neurons. There are many different ways to trigger these neurons, such as watching a ball be kicked, hearing the sound of the ball when it's kicked, or simply hearing the word kick.

These neurons have a very sophisticated firing pattern. In fact, the pattern greatly depends on the context or meaning of the action the person is watching, such as reaching your hand up to grab a ball or reaching your hand up to ask a question. Both of these actions involve the exact same muscles, but they aren't backed by the same intentions, so there will be different mirror neuron pathways triggers.

This is the reason why Iacoboni believed that there was enough complexity to the firing patterns of the neurons that it would give people the chance to understand the intent of a person depending on what the context of the action was. The presence of this process is very important when you begin thinking about how understanding and relating to others is so important to how we survive in society. This is also seen in different types of research, especially emotional contagion.

Electromagnetic Fields

Another explanation of empaths is the electromagnetic fields. This is based on the fact that the heart and brain create what is known as an electromagnetic field. According to HeartMath Institute, these fields are able to send information about the emotions and thoughts of other people. Empaths tend to be more sensitive to this input and typically find that they are overwhelmed by it. They tend to have stronger emotional and physical responses to the changes within the electromagnetic fields of the sun and earth. Empaths have a deep understanding that whatever happens to the sun and earth will also have a big impact on their energy and state of mind.

There are many different electromagnetic fields in the world and not just the ones that run within us. In September of 2015, the World Health Organization (WHO) decided to recognized electro hypersensitivity and multiple chemical sensitivity as real diseases that should be included in the International Classification of Diseases. Both of these are caused by the magnetic fields of today's technology, such as smart meters used by utility companies, microwaves, Wi-Fi, communication networks, and weather geoengineering, as well as the chemicals used in our food products.

All of these fields can have a strong impact on empaths. This is why it is important for an empath to limit their time around technology and take the time to ground themselves.

Emotional Contagion

Decades ago, Carl Jung said, "Emotions are contagious." Emotional contagion is the process of a group or person influencing the actions of other people or groups through conscious or unconscious induction of emotions and attitudes. This is a deep-rooted process of the human psyche. They have discovered that newborn infants are able to instinctively imitate the expressions of others in only minutes after being born.

Adults also have a tendency to imitate the demeanor of other people, which is typically an unconscious action. This mimicry will share emotions between individuals and plays a large role in the relationships we form with others. In fact, people tend to like those who imitate them more. It is believed that mimicry helps us to feel connected to people and provides us with a positive emotional experience. Emotional contagion is developed from this basic form of mimicry as we continue to work towards feeling loved and close to the people around us. From the moment we are born, we spontaneously register and try to recreate non-verbal language.

Emotional contagion doesn't necessarily mean empathy. Emotional contagion acts quickly, automatically, and unconsciously, and mainly relies on non-verbal communication. Empathy, on the other hand, involves a sophisticated cognitive process. There are some scholars who say that emotional contagion is a primitive type of empathy, but they also explain that it is what separates us from psychopaths. Psychopaths have the ability to use the "cognitive" parts of empathy, like looking at things from another person's perspective, but actually being impacted by a person's feelings on a feeling level doesn't happen for them.

While emotional contagion is universal, individuals have various levels of susceptibility. Every interaction has an energy dynamic that will determine which person will pull the other into an emotional orbit. The "senders" in the world are able to infect others with their emotions. Then the "catchers" in the world are the ones who are more likely to be infected with those emotions. Senders are often charismatic and dominant, while catchers tend to be attentive to the emotions of people around them.

Besides the person's natural temperament, there are other factors that play into this like moods, attention, and setting. For example, when there are obvious power differences among a group of people, like in a work situation, it is typically the influential one that sends out emotions, which sets the emotional tone for all of the other people involved.

If the team leader is happy, the rest of the group will naturally be happier. The opposite is also true.

Emotional contagion could very well explain empaths, but simply catching another person's emotions doesn't mean that you have functional and healthy empathy. If you have an unregulated emotional contagion, and everybody has this sometimes, you can end up feeling burned out and overwhelmed. After a while, you could shut down, dissociate, and numb yourself from others to protect yourself.

While science hasn't ventured quite this far, the empath experience does seem to indicate that a human process does exist where humans can innately sense and feel the emotions of other people in a way that's not completely controlled through the conscious thought process. Empaths would probably enjoy being able to switch off this ability every once and a while so that they could simply feel their own emotions. However, their experiences are largely unconscious and uncontrollable. A lot of empaths have reported that they feel overwhelmed by the emotions of others without intending to experience them.

Normally, when a person decides that they want to improve a skill, they will make a conscious decision to do it, and then they start some type of practice and begin learning what they want to. There are people who find that this process comes more naturally for them, so they may not have to practice as long. For an empath, they first have a physical manifestation. They begin by feeling what others feel, and they don't understand what is happening. It is only after this takes place that they begin to try and understand what is happening to them. A lot of empaths would have the thought of, "How can I make this stop?"

The abilities of an empath never show up as a learned skill, something that a person can wish to have and then start to grow and develop it with practice. Typically, the first trigger will be physiological, which will then move into an emotional experience and then become a conscious awareness. They feel their abilities first and begin to understand them later. They will report having no, or very little control over this process. This means that empathy is innate, yet not everybody will experience it. In fact, a very time percentage of the general population actually has this ability. Everybody can perceive a person's emotions, but only empaths are able to feel the emotional cues.

Increased Dopamine Sensitivity

One of the main neurotransmitters in the brain is dopamine. Dopamine increases the activity of neurons and is connected with the pleasure response. Research has discovered that introverted empaths tend to be more sensitive to dopamine than extroverts. This basically means that they won't need as much dopamine to be happy. This could explain the reason why they are content with practicing meditation, alone time, and reading, and they don't need to have as much external stimulation from social gatherings. Extroverts have to have that dopamine rush from social events. They can't seem to get enough of it.

In a study published in the September 2014 issue of *Social Cognitive and Affective Neuroscience*, found that lower dopamine levels were connected with higher donation amounts of money to poor children in developing nations, as well as better performance in tasks that required thinking. Humans who had higher levels are connected with better recall and recognition of positive emotional stimuli and with better cooperation in interactions. There is a connection between norepinephrine, which is created from dopamine, empathy behaviors, and the negative connection to dopamine levels and social interactions. There is a chance that an enzyme with the ability to regulate norepinephrine and dopamine levels could regulate a person's empathic abilities and behaviors.

DBH is what helps to change dopamine to norepinephrine. When DBH is inhibited, dopamine levels increase, and norepinephrine levels decrease.

Other studies have confirmed that DBH is very important to social functioning. Humans who have social dysfunctions, like patients who are autistic, tend to have lower DBH activity than the control groups.

In the study mentioned earlier, they measured a person's empathic perceptions by using what they called "reading the mind in the eyes test," where the participants recognized the emotional states of others by using cue from the eyes. To measure their response, they used a subscale in the interpersonal reactivity index. Their participants were 329 students from the Henan University of Science and Technology in China. The RMET test they took was a paper-and-pencil test that contained 36 items. Each item was a picture that showed the eye area of a Caucasian person and four adjectives to describe their emotions.

Of their participants, 59% responded accurately. Of those who responded on the subscale of having empathic reactivity, and who responded correctly on the emotions, had higher levels of DBH.

Synesthesia

Synesthesia is considered to be a neurological condition where two senses are grouped together within the brain. For example, a person is able to see a piece of music when they are listening to it, or they are able to taste words. There are a few famous synesthetics, including Billy Joel, Itzhak Perlman, and Isaac Newton. However, mirror-touch synesthesia refers to when people can feel the emotions and sensations of others in their body as if they were the one in pain.

Not all empaths are synesthetes. Mirror-touch synesthetes say that they have a tactile sensation on their self when they see another person being touched. The mirror-touch neurons were first found by Italian researchers who were studying the macaque monkey. They found that the same area of the monkey's brain lit up whether they performed a task or witnessed another monkey doing something.

Mirror-touch synesthesia could go like this. Let's say that you are working in the garden with your friend, and then she gets stung on the hand by a bee, and then you all of a sudden feel the stinging sensation on your hand. It could also be that your little sister is brought to tears because she lost her best friend, you can't help but cry too.

This form of synesthesia is typically a developmental disorder, but it has also affected people who have lost an extremity. Some people have hyperactive somatosensory mirror systems, which causes them to feel what others feel. We have receptors all over our bodies, and they are connected with the neurons in the central nervous system.

The severity of this will vary between individuals, with some barely being able to notice a feeling and others feeling things so strongly they are debilitated by it. Some professionals believe that this is a genetic condition. In order to be diagnosed with mirror-touch synesthesia, you have to meet two criteria:

1. An unconscious sensation or synesthetic response to what you see another person experience.

2. Higher levels of empathy.

In the majority of studies, people were asked to watch another person be touched and say whether or not they experienced a synesthetic response and what it felt like. They discovered that the object that was used to touch the other person was important. They found that if the object they used was hard or solid, the sensation was often stronger than if the object used was soft.

Medical experts could pinpoint the difference in the central nervous system and brain of people with mirror-touch synesthesia. To figure out brain activity, they used fMRI or transcranial direct current stimulation. Besides feeling only touched, mirror-touch synesthetes can feel emotions. Empaths who have mirror-touch synesthesia tend to have stronger levels of empathy than empaths who do not.

Chapter 3: Making Sense Of Old Wounds

We empaths are sensitive souls. We feel things so strong that they become a part of who we are. We are the wounded healers of the world. We can help everyone else, except our self. Heartbreak plays a big part in our world. To heal from it, the brokenness has to be faced. I can't speak for everybody, but I have come up with a theory that applies to many empaths.

At some point in an empath's life, their heart gets broken. This heartbreak teaches you that you don't deserve to be loved. Something happened in life, and the only logical conclusion that you could make was that you don't deserve the love that you want. Why else would the universe deny it to you?

Hopefully, as an adult, you started to realize that not receiving love didn't mean that you don't deserve love. Not everybody in this world has the capacity to give love. It's like thinking that you aren't worthy of being held when you live with birds. Birds don’t have arms to be able to hold you; it has nothing to do with you.

No matter how much you rationalize things, once you have formed the belief, it will become a subconscious pattern. You expect that nobody is going to love you, and you start trying to “prove” to people that you are worthy of it, with the hopes of being awarded the love you want.

You also learn that the only way to feel love is to love someone else. When you love somebody, you are able to experience that same love just a bit. While you are giving, you get to feel the love within yourself, and it feels amazing. This makes you want to continue to give more and more.

This will create a pattern of co-dependence. This means you set yourself in the role of a giver, and you attract takers, such as narcissists, into your life. You become stuck in the pattern of giving endlessly and deplete yourself more. This causes you to start panicking that you aren't giving enough of yourself and proving that you are worthy of love. No matter what you do, you still don't feel worthy. The reason for this, whatever you can and can't do, doesn't change these assumptions. The belief that you are unworthy needs to be gotten rid of on a deep subconscious level so that you can heal your self-image. You don't need to continue playing this game.

Why is this important? Because empaths who have been broken tend to devalue themselves, and they continue to kill themselves in order to "earn" the love of others. It feels like the "obvious" choice, yet when you understand the underlying programming that you start to see the solution isn't giving more. Instead, you have to shift the pattern of totally giving to something that is balanced. You do this by:

- Learning the best way to take care of yourself and don’t take care of others as much.
- Meet other givers.
- Learn to create boundaries with the takers.

- Learn how to get rid of your unworthiness programming.

Now, at this point, you may be thinking this is all fine and dandy, but how did I end up broken? That's a valid question and one that you really need to find the answer to. Every empath will face their own hurt, so you will have to figure out exactly where yours came from, I can't tell you that, but there are commonalities amongst our hurt, and the biggest being narcissistic parents.

Narcissistic Parents

Anybody can be faced with narcissistic parents, not just empaths, and they are just as damaging. Narcissists are bad for anybody they get their claws into, but for empaths, things tend to be much worse. All children need to be nurtured as they grow so that they become well-adjusted adults, but narcissists don’t have that capability. For the empath, this can be a much bigger problem.

I want to share something I saw at a store one day. There was a young girl, couldn't have been older than three, who started crying because her mom told her she couldn't have a toy. Her mom was immediately upset and snapped, "I don't have time for your nonsense. Why do you act like this when I'm in a hurry? You know how to ruin my day". This hurt my heart. It wasn't because her mom had told her no when it came to the toy, but because the mom cared more about her own feelings that she could feel any empathy for her child. The less narcissistic mother would have empathized with their child and said something like, "I understand you want that toy, but you've already got some fun things in the buggy", or something like that. They wouldn't have dumped their own feelings on the little girl, and the tantrum would have likely subsided.

Throughout your childhood, when raised by a narcissist, you start to develop the belief that you aren't "good enough" despite everything you try to do and bending over backward to try and make others happy. It kills your boundaries, which are the invisible barriers everybody needs to have between them and the outside world. These are what help to regulate the flow of information between you and these outside things. Damaged boundaries prevent you from being able to communicate powerfully and authentically. It also hurts your self-concept, which will also hurt your relationships and your ability to thrive in the world. The majority of grown-up children of narcissists never seek the help they need to heal from this because they don't realize that their childhood was destructive and unhealthy.

As you know, I've had a lot of personal experience with narcissistic parents, specifically with my mother. I can tell you that if you had a narcissistic parent, your boundaries aren't where they should be for you to live a confident, healthy, and happy life.

Children of narcissists end to be unable to see good in themselves, deeply insecure, overly sensitive, which as empaths, we don't need any more of to feel unlovable and unworthy. And since they have become familiar with narcissism, they will end up attracting more of it into their life, in their careers and relationships.

We've talked a lot about narcissism already, but let's back up for a moment and define what narcissism is and isn't. The word narcissist has been used a lot to describe anybody who is self-centered, vain, likes to be the center of attention, or arrogant. This isn't the narcissism we are talking about, and those people wouldn't technically be considered narcissists unless they show some of the actions we will discuss.

Narcissistic personality disorder is a mental disorder. People with this disorder suffer from an inflated sense of self-importance, a lack of empathy, and a strong need for admiration. Behind all of this is lies a very fragile self-esteem that will get hurt with the slightest bit of criticism.

NPD causes issues in their finances, school, work, and relationships. They become very disappointed and unhappy when they don't receive the admiration or special favors that they think they should get. Others typically don't like being around those with NPD, and most of their relationships are going to be unfulfilling.

Some recent studies have discovered that six percent of the population has suffered from clinical NPD at some point, but there are more people who have non-clinical symptoms. I personally feel that the number seems to be a bit low. I've met quite a few adult children of narcissists.

We are getting ready to go over the signs and hallmarks that you could have been raised by a narcissist, but it is very important for your wellbeing that you don't start blaming or hating your parents if they are or have been a narcissist. Everybody in life is only trying to do the best they can, and they likely suffer from this disorder because of their own harmful childhood that they need to heal from but was never able to. We aren't trying to blame anyone, but instead, we are simply shedding some like on the problem so that if you have been raised by a narcissist, you are able to recognize the issue and get help.

There are general traits of a narcissist, but I want to look at specifics when it comes to being parented by a narcissist, such they demand you to agree with them, or they will reject you. This is why a lot of adult children of narcissists experience conditional love. They have to meet a certain condition of the parent in order to get love in return. This plays into what we talked about at the beginning of the chapter. We think we have to do something in order for somebody to love us, but that's not the case. Love is meant to be unconditional. You love somebody because you want to, not because they did something for you.

Now, I want to explain that there are two types of narcissists. First is healthy narcissism. This is where you have good self-esteem, believe in yourself, and you have a realistic self-evaluation. These people can empathize with others, and they are able to take criticisms and failures. Second is the malignant narcissist. These are the troublesome narcissists that we are talking about. They have to have praise at all times and don't take criticism very well.

So, let's take a look at some parenting specifics that you may have experienced during your childhood, and possibly during your adulthood. These exist on a spectrum, and most narcissistic parents won't have all of these.

1. They want to present a perfect family to the outside world. Your parents went to amazing lengths to try and make sure that others saw you as a loving or successful family. You were probably aware of this, but you didn't say anything.

2. They were always right and never ever wrong. Even if they did make a mistake or treated you unfairly, they wouldn't apologize. If you confronted them, they would deny it and somehow blame you.

3. They were never empathetic. They wouldn't ask you how you felt or sympathize with you.

4. They would project their bad actions onto you. For example, if you had an argument with them, the narcissistic parent would yell at you and say something like, "How dare you to scream at me like that? Go to your room, and don't come out until you can learn to stop screaming at me."

5. They would react extremely to any type of criticism. Did you ever criticize them? How would they react? They probably acted in an extreme way. They probably screamed, and probably tried to hurt you in some way.

6. If there was more than one child, they had a favorite child. They likely had a "golden" and a "scapegoat" child. This meant one couldn't do any harm, while the other was the black sheep and caused all of the problems.

7. They treated you like the parent. This is known as being parentified. They expected you to "parent" the parent, or act as a surrogate parent to cater to whatever they needed.

8. They would gaslight you. To control you, they would use psychological manipulation, specifically gaslighting. This means that they are trying to make you feel crazy or doubt your sanity so that they could keep the upper hand.

9. They exert explicit control. Basically, if you didn't do exactly what they wanted, they would punish you in some way.

10. They would insult you. Narcissistic parents like to harass, demean, and berate you.

11. They didn't listen or care about how you felt. You felt as if you couldn't be honest with them. Whatever issue you had, they would spin it into a pity party for them.

12. They would lie to you. Narcissistic parents lie to control and manipulate you. You never really knew what you could trust.

13. They would "own" your accomplishments. If you got a compliment about something you achieved, your narcissistic parent would jump in and turn the attention on themselves. They would say things like, "They get that from me".

14. They would compete with you. If you were able to get something nice for yourself, they would take it or try to get something better.

15. They refused to respect your boundaries. You didn't have a "private" space. They would go through your things, just trying to find something to use against you.

16. They would always try to "get even". If you did anything, they saw as "wrong",even if it was tiny, they would always punish you. This

childish act of getting even could have been obvious or subtle.

17. They loved you when you did as they wanted. Your parents would take love away quickly. If you didn't do as they asked, they would punish you or give you the cold shoulder.

18. They were great at the guilt trip. This was another way to control you.

19. They would try to control you with codependency. You heard things like, "I need you; don't leave me." This prevented you to live your own life or create independent priorities.

When it comes to the empathic child, they can pick up on the emotional vulnerability of their parents. They will start to compliment them or try to be a reflection of them. They do this with the hopes of taking care of their parents so that, eventually, their parents will take care of them. This causes them to lose touch with who they are.

Narcissistic Siblings

Children of narcissists tend to go in one of two directions. They either become a narcissist, or they become co-dependent. Empaths are more likely to become the latter. This also means that if an empath has siblings, there is a good chance they have to face being bullied by a narcissistic sibling. This can happen, though not very often, even if their parents aren't narcissistic.

Children who grow up in dysfunctional households don't often have close relationships with siblings. They will often continue the abuse throughout their adulthood. Siblings are normally forced to compete for attention and love, and they often forced to turn on each other. As an empath, you have to make sure you protect yourself from your sibling that wants to "take you out." You have probably asked yourself, "Why would they want to hurt me?" Very simple, narcissistic siblings don't have any feelings, and they are likely envious of you, or they simply want to be in control of the family.

As the empath, you were likely faced with the role of the scapegoat, and you were subjected to the brunt of their "attention." The scapegoat has already been subjected to a lot of abuse, and they tend to be the most intelligent, and this causes their sibling to feel threatened. These are some of the most classic signs that you have a narcissistic sibling:

1. You don't understand why, but you always feel uneasy when you are around them.

2. They are extremely manipulative.

3. They are critical of whatever you do.

4. They share your secrets with other family members, or they tell them lies about you.

5. They feign concern and will try to make you feel guilty if you don't have their back.

6. They will make the rest of the family think you are mentally unstable or crazy.

7. They will constantly put themselves in competition with you. You often notice they are jealous, and they may even flirt with your partner or date.

8. They try to steal your friends and may try to hurt your relationships with other family members.

9. They are great at playing the victim and tend to act passive-aggressively.

10. You feel as if they are judging you, always.

11. You feel as if they are always prying into your personal life, trying to dig up information.

12. They are always lying, and if you call them out, they will twist it.

13. You feel exhausted when you have to deal with them. They are great at sucking the life out of you.

Siblings like this will do anything and everything to destroy you. Some will even go so far as to involve the police. They don't care, and the scary part, which is true for narcissistic parents as well, is they don't even realize they are doing anything wrong. They sincerely believe that they are the perfect one, and you are the bad one trying to hurt them.

Before we move into the next section, I want to reiterate something. I mentioned in the parent section that you shouldn't start blaming or hating any narcissistic person you discover in your life. As I said, they are doing the best with what they have. But, having said that, that doesn't mean you have to put up with it. If you go through the rest of your life making excuses for them and allowing them to continue to hurt you, you will continue to have a co-dependent relationship with them, and you will never be able to heal. While they don't know anybody, you do. It is okay to cut them out of your life. Just because they are family does not mean you have to let them have a role in your life.

Friendships

As an empath, you have probably struggled with friendships. As empaths, we have learned that society doesn't like our sensitivity. As such, we have learned to cloak it under a guise of indifference and independence. We tend to seek out validation for our sensitivities and are pulled towards "project friends." These are people who are emotionally off-kilter, and they need attention and help. Our need for approval causes us to get into abusive or co-dependent relationships.

Since we are the world's natural healers, we are pulled towards unstable and wounded people. The inexperienced empath has to learn how to distinguish between their energy and the energy of others and stop trying to help those they are emotionally pulled towards. Everybody is responsible for their own emotions, empaths, or not.

Even when we start a friendship with a person who isn’t in need of help, we tend to self-sabotage the relationship. In this case, it has more to do with us than them. This also makes it hard for us to establish a healthy romantic relationship.

Here are a few problems that we are faced with in friendships:

1. We want a reciprocated friendship. Empaths want a friend to be just as into the friendship as they are, and this can lead to problems. We may be very in tune with emotions, but we sometimes get too much into the emotion to realize that friendships don't have to be perfect.

2. We invest way more into the friendship than we receive. Empaths are givers, as we have established, and we don't know when to stop, and that is exhausting not only to us but to our friends as well.

3. Exhaustion can cause us to become angry. Anybody would get angry if they feel like they are giving all they have without seeing a

return from the other side. The problem is, our friends don’t ask us to give that much of our self, so it isn’t their job to reciprocate.

4. Empaths know what their needs are, but they aren’t that great at sharing them. We are more used to giving, so we aren’t great at letting our friends know what we need out of the relationship, and this plays into all of the other points I have made.

5. We need open conversations. This can be a problem because sometimes people don’t feel comfortable being completely open, even with close friends.

6. We need to trust our friends, and we want our friends to trust us. While this may seem completely normal, people who aren't empaths find it easier to trust others because they aren't always plugged into their emotions.

7. Empaths need honest friends. As human lie detectors, if our friend isn’t honest, we know it. As you can imagine, this causes quite a few problems.

To have a healthy friendship, we have to learn how to separate ourselves from our friend's emotions. Otherwise, we are going to be exhausted, overloaded, or anxious constantly. Empaths tend to avoid relationships of any kind because they are afraid that they are going to be engulfed in these emotions. As empaths, we want companionship, but we don't see it as safe.

In order to establish healthy relationships, you have to learn how to assert your own personal needs. This includes physical limits and time limits. You won't be able to have emotional freedom with another person until you can do this. Everybody has an invisible energetic border, and as an empath, yours will likely be bigger than others. Learn what your space is, and you will be able to establish better boundaries so that you can have healthy friendships and other relationships.

Chapter 4: Dealing With Anxiety And Chronic Fatigue

As we are all very aware, being an empath comes with many challenges. One of those challenges is having to live with heightened sensitivities, such as intolerances and allergies. While many empaths are used to this, you may reach a certain age where these sensitivities go into overdrive.

There are lots of different reasons for this, but it all comes down to compromised immune systems and changing hormones. This normally happens around the mid-thirties. But even before then, empaths can struggle with chronic fatigue and anxiety.

Science has proven that empaths are more prone to anxiety, depression, and social anxiety. Out hypersensitivity to emotions can cause us to become ill, as well, and suffer from stress, burnout in our jobs, and suffer actual pain more than others. This brings me to the point of jobs for empaths. I'm sure school was hard because you were constantly surrounded by others, but now you're an adult, and jobs are the new crowded space you have to face.

The Hidden Workplace Dynamics

First off, the corporate culture in America is fairly universal. Once you have worked in one corporate place, you can understand another. Secondly, it is messed up. Think about this for a moment. In the corporate world, you are supposed to work being your number one priority. Even places who promise a work-home balance would like for you to lean more toward work, admonishing people for being sick or taking care of their children. It is almost as if they want you to come to work sick and pass it along.

It seems as if the management is less qualified than those who are doing the actual work. I'm not saying they are all unqualified, but there are a lot of managers out there who don't seem to truly know what their employees actually do, don't follow the same schedules and rules they have for their staff, and often suffer from control or ego issues that make them a bad choice for handling employees.

Then you have conflict at work. That's a complete nightmare. There is supposed to be a system to help you handle a hostile work environment. There is a chain of command where problems are reported and an HR department to speak with when this can't be resolved. Yet, when you report a problem, you become the problem.

I speak from experience. At one of my first big jobs, I was exposed to repeated harassment from a coworker. Not only did I find it emotionally challenging to face, but it also kept me from doing my job. I talked to my supervisor about the problem, which had been witnessed by them and every other coworker at some point. It happened every day, and I worked my way up the chain to fix this. Once I was to management, I was informed it was a female problem.

Basically, women are catty, so I should just expect this treatment. First off, this hadn't really been something I had experience with other women before. Second, this is something that is learned and isn't something that should be allowed in the workplace. Third, it is sexist even to suggest that a harassment issue is a gender problem that doesn't deserve to be taken seriously.

Things continued until I had to be moved to a different department. But I had a little note placed into my file saying that I had issues with conflict resolution. At this point, I had already started going to therapy, which is why I went to my supervisor; otherwise, I would have never spoken up. I didn't have an issue with resolving conflicts. My issue was being in a hostile work environment, and having a coworker be allowed to terrorize me with no repercussions. After I left her department, she found a new target, which was a man, and it couldn't be written off as a female thing and was soon fired.

This left me feeling horrible, and I questioned the point of reporting harassment and if I had been in the wrong for reporting it. I wondered why this continued to follow me through on every performance review, impacting my salary and movement in the company.

A lot of people will face problems like this, but empaths in the corporate world will absorb these negative energies. When we do the right thing, it will always feel wrong because we get gaslighted by those who should be helping. We get told that we are the issue and are often labeled as a troublemaker for addressing ethical issues or harassment. They just want us to sit quietly and do our job.

Since empaths are strongly impacted by energy, we absorb all of that toxic work culture. This causes us to feel as if we really are in the wrong because if we are so impacted by what others say, we simply need to just get over it. Our sense of ethics tells us we need to fix this, but our boss is telling us to get over it and ignore it. This doesn't feel congruent with us.

This unbalanced workplace is upsetting, and we internalize all of this.

If you are a female empath, you get hit with misogyny as well. Women are supposed to just be friendly and nice and are criticized if they try to stand up for themselves. When a problem arises, they do their best to make us believe we are the problem, and as an empath, we believe that wholeheartedly. I believe, though, that these situations may be a nudge from the Universe. It's telling us we are in a job that we shouldn't be. When we feel drained and unfulfilled, we have to be willing to get ourselves out of that situation, but we sometimes find that hard. So, we have to face this hostile work environment so that we feel at least a little bit okay with quitting.

The following are just a few more specific ways where empaths can find problems when working in an unfulfilling job.

1. Empaths may end up revealing too much. If somebody makes an empath feel the least bit

safe, they will sometimes start sharing things that are then used against them. This can have some severe repercussions and can attract their narcissistic colleagues and alienate the colleagues that aren't.

2. We know that we are attracted to needy people, and there are needy people everywhere. When an empath creates an alliance with a needy colleague, it can drain their energy, cause them to feel terrible, and reinforces their misconceptions about reality,

3. Empaths also don't do a good job at saying no, so we are placed in a position where we end up saying yes all the time. This means that we end up being the dumping ground for the work other people don't want to do because we can't tell them no.

4. Following that last point, we will also work, work, and work some more in the hopes that people will reward us and appreciate us.

We've likely been taught that in order for people to like us that we have to do things for them. The problem is, we won't get the recognition or reward that we expect in the corporate world.

5. Lastly, empaths may play it too safe. They are afraid of putting themselves out there, or they believe that they can't do something more, so it leaves them in a position where they just have to suffer through.

Why Work Leaves Me Tired

Empaths need to make sure their job works with their empathic gifts and won't drain them. The number one job that empaths should never be in is a sales job. Most empaths will find this unfulfilling, especially if you are more introverted. Having to deal with the public will take a lot out of yours. There are a lot of emotions in jobs like this, and empaths will find this very hard to handle. Soaking in all of these emotions will leave you feeling tired, anxious, and all-around sick. Add in the bright lights, speakers, and people talking incessantly; you’re not going to have the energy to take care of yourself.

Some other extremely stressful and unfulfilling careers include trial attorneys, an executive for large teams, politics, and public relations. These jobs require extroversion, being able to engage in small talk, and aggressiveness and not a person who tends to be introspective, sensitive, and soft-spoken.

The mainstream corporate world is also a bad idea. Having to follow the rules of the corporate world is hard for empaths. This type of structure has always confused and frustrated me because it doesn't give you any place to go, and it doesn't care about a person's needs. Empaths are thinkers, and they will question the status quo if things don't feel right to them. They want to know the "whys" behind the decisions so that everything makes sense to them. Plus, power-hungry coworkers and regular team meetings tend to drain empaths, who tend to function better when they work on their own.

Workplaces are full of tension, as I'm sure you're aware of, and as empaths, we try to block all of this tension. When we do this, it leaves us contracted. This constant contraction drains us of all of our energy. We go home feeling miserable, and if you are stuck in an unhealthy relationship, that causes even more problems.

Even if you are in a job that isn't ideal for an empath and you aren't at a place where you could leave, there are ways you and improve your situation so that it is more comfortable. When an empath is happy at work, they are able to flourish and make great contributions to their job.

If you have the ability to do so now, it is a good idea to get into a career that is rewarding for empaths. Empaths tend to be happier in a low stress, solo jobs, or working for small companies. They like it when they are able to work at least partly at home so that they can be away from the frenzy at the office, the politics, and the energy vampires. Jobs like this allow you to plan out your schedule and take breaks when needed in order to decompress.

A lot of empaths like to be self-employed so that they can avoid the overwhelm and drain of packed schedules, coworkers, and bosses. Empaths often do a lot better on their own time than if they have to go to team meetings that are often required when working for large corporations.

If you do work for a business, see if there is a change that you can arrange for some of you work to be done at home, and do what you can virtually through Skype, texts, emails, and internet. It has become increasingly popular for people not to have to be tied to their office in order to do their job, which is a perk for empaths that gives us more choices for our work location. However, if you do choose to work from home or alone in an office, make sure you don't allow yourself to become totally isolated or try to push yourself too hard. You need to try to balance you alone time with some time with people.

So how can you take these considerations and put them into a job? Empaths will feel satisfied as self-employed business owners, artists, health care professionals, editors, writers, and other creative careers. There are a lot of musicians and actors who have said they are "highly sensitive," such as Jim Carrey, Alanis Morissette, Claire Danes, and Scarlet Johansson.

Some other good options are independent plumbers and electricians, lawyers, or accounts with home offices, virtual assistants, and graphic and website designers. You could also be a business consultant or a real estate agent as long as you make sure that you establish clear boundaries regarding when somebody can contact you and make sure you don't over-schedule yourself. Forest ranger, gardener, landscape design, or other jobs that place you in nature are also great choices for empaths.

There are a lot of empaths who also choose to help professions because they like helping others. This could include jobs like a psychiatrist, non-profit employee, life coaches, hospice workers, clergy, massage therapists, Chinese medical practitioners, yoga instructors, teachers, social workers, psychotherapists, physical therapists, dentists, nurses, or physicians. The important thing is to remember that you need to take care of your energy and not take on the stress of your patients. Some other gratifying choices are veterinary medicine, dog grooming, and animal rescue.

If you are an empath who chooses a helping profession, you have to learn to quit taking on the symptoms and stress of those you are helping. This can be done through scheduling breaks between clients so that you meditate, and make sure you set boundaries with people. Take a short walk outside every now and then to help you refuel and relax. However, jobs like firefighter or police officer, no matter how much you can help people in these positions, tend to be too stressful for an empath and will place you in a high sensory situation.

Empaths are extremely valuable in all types of careers. However, you have to find a job that supports your gifts, temperament, and skills. The attributes of an empath may not be as appreciated in areas like government, military, professional sports, academia, or corporations. Better matches include the arts and business with humanistic awareness. When you are looking at jobs, make sure you use your intuition to figure out if you would be a good fit for that company's goals and mission. Also, get a feel for the energy of the space and people. While a job may look right on paper, it may not be right for you.

Healing Exercises

Whether you are in a job that works with your abilities or not, there are still going to be times when you start feeling stressed. But we are going to go over some exercises that you can do that will help you to make your work less stressful, set better boundaries, and feel better all-around when it comes to your job.

1. Rate Your Tasks

Take a look at the work that you have to do each day. Write them all down and then go through and rate them between one and five as to how draining they are, one being not draining and five being completely draining. Having this information will help you to plan your day with how your energy naturally flows.

2. Getting Rid of Tasks

Of the exhausting tasks you have on your list, try to figure out if there is a way that you can get rid of those tasks. Is there somebody else that you can ask to do them? Were they supposed to be your task, to begin with, or did somebody ask you to do it? If you can't get rid of them totally, is there anything you can do to reduce them, so they aren't as exhausting? Can they be broken down into smaller tasks that you can do throughout the day? Anything that will provide you with time to relax a bit.

3. Getting Energizing Tasks

From the list you made at the beginning, those ones and twos on your list would also be considered the most energizing tasks that you do. Now, is there anything you can do to get more those tasks and fewer of the fours and fives? Maybe you could work out a deal with a coworker. There could be somebody else that hates doing the task you find energizing, so tell them if they do what you don't like, you will take the tasks they don't like. You can also speak with your supervisor to see if there is anything they can do.

A lot of this will mean that you have to step out of your comfort zone. And outside of your comfort zone is where you grow. So, speak up and talk to your boss and coworkers. Learn to say no, and delegate tasks that you know will cause you to feel exhausted.

Aside from these steps, here are some other things you can do to limit the exhaustiveness of your job.

1. Learn How to Disconnect

Just being around others drain empaths. Try to give yourself some alone time so that you can recharge and get out of all of that energy. It's important that you learn not to take everything personally. You need to learn how to discern. Discernment means you detach from emotions in interactions, decisions, or situations with others. Take a step back. Look at the situation for what it really is, and then bring that emotional attachment back into you. If you make a point to do this every day, it can change the outlook you have about your career.

2. Look at the End

Empaths who haven't quite mastered or recognized their abilities will often feel negative in the present. Instead of seeing tasks as negative, view them as positive outcomes. Try to focus on the things that you want to achieve without allowing yourself to become emotionally connected to the achievements of others.

3. Be Proud of Who You Are

Even if you don't have an empath friendly job, try to find ways you can use your gift to make your workplace a better place. You can feel how others are feeling, so use your abilities to change energy by shifting yours. Try to find the soulful and emotional moments of business interactions, meetings, and coworkers. Also, make sure that you check in with your emotions so that you know you block out the negative invasions. Use your abilities so that you are proactive and ready for anything.

4. Serve Your Needs

Quit serving others at your own detriment. You have to make sure you come first and recharge when you need to. You need to connect with nature in whatever way you can. Take your lunch outside. Have a houseplant on your desk if you're allowed to.

Find ways to improve your spiritual and mental health while at work, and when you are asked to help somebody else, you will be ready to do so.

Chapter 5: Eliminating Negative Energies From Narcissists And Energy Vampires

We've talked about the issues empaths have with narcissists, specifically within their families. But this issue doesn't stop there. Narcissists search out the "weak" people in that world that they can easily control, and the empaths seem to be the perfect mark. Narcissists aren't the only problem. There are also energy vampires. In this chapter, we will talk about the issues with both and how you can protect and heal yourself from these energy stealing beings.

Downward Spiral With Narcissists

We've all heard the saying, "opposites attract." While this is typically presented to help broaden a person's horizons, people who are complete opposites could end up being brought together for the wrong reasons. For example, a narcissist is pulled to people who they can get the most use from. This normally means empaths.

Empaths are polar opposites of narcissists. People who suffer from narcissistic personality disorder have no empathy at all, and empaths are full of it. The "emotional sponges" we are seen to be are very attractive to narcissists because we are seen as somebody who will fulfill all of their needs.

This is a very toxic attraction and is a recipe for disaster. To a narcissist, empaths are loving and giving people who will be completely and utterly devoted to them and will listen and love them. The empath is attracted to a narcissist because they will see their false self-first. Narcissists have created a very good façade that they show the world where they come off as intelligent and charming and even a little giving. But that all stops once you quit doing things the way the like, and then they become punishing and cold.

While a narcissist is trying to hook somebody into their grasp, they will start out being attentive and loving, but that will start to fail. At first, empaths will only see good qualities, and they believe that the relationship will look good. This won't stay true for long because narcissists have a lot of contempt, and they very everybody as less than them. When they start to see the flaws of their partner, they won't idealize them any longer, and they begin blaming them for not being a perfect person.

There are also times where it takes a long time for their real colors to shine through, so it's best just to avoid narcissists altogether. But this proves very hard for empaths because it goes against our instincts. We believe that we can fix people and heal all things through compassion.

We question things and say things like, "If they just listened, or if they would just give a little," but that doesn't happen when it comes to a narcissist. It's really hard for empaths to believe that a person couldn't have some empathy and that they aren't able to help them with their love.

Empaths like to find harmony, but narcissists don't want harmony. They thrive in utter chaos, and they like to see how much they can pull other's strings.

Narcissists will string the empath along with bits of hope. They will add kindness and compliments into their actions, making the empath think that if they act a certain way, they will be treated with love.

As empaths, we tend to understand that everybody is just human and that all humans have defects, so we have patience in hopes that the other person will grow. And if they meet a narcissist who is willing to admit fault, even for a second, they will stick with them for a long time, but the narcissist will never follow through on making a change.

This is just a tactic they use to pull the empath back in. This is a very effective tactic for empaths because they want to be supportive and help them out. But they are ultimately exploited even more.

The pull and push in this type of relationship create a trauma bond between the abuser and the victim. This bond makes the victim feel as if it is impossible to get out of the relationship. No matter what they do, the damage is being done.

Since we are empaths, we have the willingness and ability to take a look at our self and our faults. And when there is a trauma bond, this is taken advantage of. For an empath who has been trauma bonded, it becomes a cycle because they begin to look at themselves, the things they need to change, and what they should do differently, and their characters as flaws. This is the perfect situation for the narcissist.

It's pretty hard to comprehend the fact that you're in a narcissistic relationship, but there are a lot of red flags that you can pay attention to as you start to get to know a person. The best way to keep yourself away from narcissistic abuse is to understand you are responsible for your own growth, and everybody else is responsible for their own.

Instead of telling you to "protect" yourself from the narcissist, which can be disempowering, I'm going to tell you how to spot a narcissist. The more you are consciously aware of them, the better you will be able to act around them so that they can't take control.

Interestingly enough, there are actually two types of narcissists. The first is vulnerable to narcissists. These narcissists are shy or quiet and very sensitive, but to cover their feelings of self-loathing, these narcissists will overcompensate by putting up a grandiose mask in the hopes of merging who they are with idealized people. They have an unshakeable urge to feel special, and they don't have much regard for how other people feel. They are motivated by their fear of abandonment and rejection. This means they don't have the capacity to actually care and love for other people. They like to use emotional manipulation to make sure they get attention and sympathy from others. They are full of inferiority complexes, which typically come from childhood mistreatments.

Then there are the invulnerable narcissists. These narcissists are the traditional image of them. They are the unemphatic, cold, and self-confident person. These people are thick-skinned, and they shamelessly seek pleasure, recognition, glory, and power. They suffer from god complexes and believe that they are far superior to everybody else. They also have a pathological need to let everybody know that.

Both types of narcissists have similar traits, like using others to feed their delusions, unfaithfulness, need for power, lack of empathy, criticizing ,and blaming.

The IN and VN narcissist types can also be broken down into subtypes. While unofficial subtypes, they can help you in dealing with them. As you will see, many of these overlap.

First up is the amorous narcissist. They measure their grandiosity and self-worth by how many sexual conquests they experience. They are known for their charm to hook people by using gifts and flattery, but then they get rid of them once they see them as boring and once they have met the needs of the narcissist, which often as to do with sex or status. These narcissists are the ultimate relationship con artists, heartbreakers, and "gold diggers." They will, at first, seem amiable, alluring, and attractive, but under all of that, they want to please their own desires and needs.

Next is the compensatory narcissist. They are driven by their need to compensate for past traumas. They like creating larger-than-life illusions of who they are and what they have achieved. To regain control and power in life, they will look for vulnerable people who will act as an audience to their fake stage acts. These narcissists are extremely sensitive to any type of criticism and will often look for negative self-directed cues from other people. Manipulation and emotional abuse are common control methods used by this narcissist.

Next is the elitist narcissist. This type of narcissist will do anything to get to the top and dominate others. They are convinced that they do everything better than others, often because of their backgrounds or achievements, or just because they are born that way, and this means they should be treated differently. Their sense of entitlement is seen in every area of their life, from family to work. Since they have such a large ego, they are great at one-uppers, braggers, and self-promoters. They are cut-throat at being the best and proving that they are intellectually superior all of the time and at any cost.

The last is the malignant narcissist. These narcissists' actions will often overlap those of psychopaths and people with an antisocial personality disorder. They have very little interest in what is moral or immoral, and they never feel any remorse. They are often characterized as arrogant and with an inflated sense of worth that loves to outsmart other people. You can see these narcissists in drug rehab centers, gangs, and prisons, but many will manage to "outsmart" the law.

Feeding Off The Empath's Life Force

The next beast that empaths have to face are energy vampires. Energy vampires ooze negative energy that will leave you drained. They can be intentionally malicious, or they can be oblivious to the effect they have on people. Some can be obnoxious and overbearing, while others are charming and friendly. Let's say you are at a party and talking to somebody that is nice, but suddenly you start to feel weak or nauseous. Maybe you have a coworker who constantly drones on about how they just broke with their significant other for the tenth time. Eventually, they have cheered up, but you feel utterly exhausted. The point is, these people will suck your energy dry.

While you may feel the urge to feel resentful towards these people, you need to remember that they have yet to develop the capacity to handle their issues. They prey on people because they are hurt. But you also have to remember that you aren't responsible for fixing their problems. Only they can figure out their struggles.

There are different types of energy vampires and knowing each type will help you to protect yourself.

1. Martyr or Victim

These vampires prey off of your guilt. They think people are “at the mercy” of the world. Instead of taking responsibility for their life, they emotionally blackmail, blame, and manipulate people. Their actions are caused by their low self-esteem. If they aren’t constantly receiving approval, love, and thanks, they will feel unacceptable and unworthy, which can cause them to suck away your empathy.

When you are around these people, always be on the lookout for self-pity cues. For example, this could be them blaming another person for their troubles or describing how horrible their day was. Don't let yourself get involved in this pity party. Limit your amount of interactions with them, if at all possible.

2. Narcissist

We've talked about narcissists, and they are definitely energy vampires. They are always first, and you will always be second. They expect you to put their needs first and feed their egos. They manipulate with false charm but will also stab you in the back.

If you can't completely cut this person out of your life, you need to limit how many contacts you have with them.

3. Dominator

These vampires like it when they feel superior and are the alpha. They overcompensate for their insecurities of being wrong or weak by intimidating others. They are often loud-mouthed with rigid beliefs and view the world as black and white. They tend to be bigoted, racist, and sexist.

With these vampires, you must agree to disagree. You will need to practice assertiveness when you need to and limit how many contacts you have with them. Remember that they will try to scare you, but this is from their fear of being dominated and hurt.

4. Melodramatic

These vampires thrive on causing problems. Often, this need to have constant drama is caused by an underlying emptiness. They seek out crisis because it gives them a chance to play the victim, avoid real issues, and exaggerate their sense of importance. They feed off of these negative emotions because these emotions are addictive.

When dealing with this type of vampire, refuse to take sides or play a part in their pot-stirring. Look for the patterns in their actions and the triggers that cause you to want to help. Cut them out if you can, but at least make sure you keep them at a distance.

5. Judgmental

Since the judgmental vampire has low self-worth, they love to pick on others. The way they treat people is simply a reflection of the way they treat themselves. They like to prey on a person's insecurities and boost their ego by making people feel ashamed, small, or pathetic.

When dealing with these people, keep in mind that real self-worth comes from within. Don't take what they say personally. Remember that they have deep pain, and they have a need to feel good about themselves. If you allow yourself to get defensive, you will lose. Do your best to keep a balanced head and be sweet because this will throw them off the game. As always, reduce your interactions with them.

6. Innocent

Not every energy vampire is malicious, and this is true for the innocent vampire. Sometimes energy vampires can simply be a helpless person who actually needs help like a good friend or a child who ends up relying on you too much. It's good to help somebody, but you also need to encourage them to be self-sufficient. Always being their rock is going to erode away your energy. You have to make sure that you save some energy to support yourself.

To protect your energy, it is great to show help people, but you also have to love yourself. Remind the innocent vampire that you also have to have time for yourself. Encourage them to create resilience, strength, and fortitude so that you will be able to step out of the giver role.

I've given you bits of information on how to protect yourself from these different types of energy vampires, but I'm going to give you some more information. You can never be too careful when you are dealing with these types of people.

1. Don't be the accountable one. They are charismatic, so they can slink out of trouble with ease. They are great at pinning problems on other people. They don't like accepting culpability for the role they played in a problem, and you will often be the one with the guilt and blame. Don't let this happen. Tell your side so that people know the role you played, and the part played by the other person.

2. Start a journal where you keep track of your gut instincts. This may sound odd, but a big part of being empath is learning to follow your gut instincts. This can be helpful when it comes to spotting the energy vampires in your life. If you are constantly writing about a certain person and how they spark a negative feeling in your instinct, then they may be somebody you need to cut out of your life.

3. Find a friend that you really trust that you can get a reality-check from. The important part is to make sure this is a person that you trust and who you know will be honest with you. They are the person that will tell you when you are running yourself thin. They will be honest about the new person you are hanging out with and how they are bad for you.

4. Make sure you say no. The only way energy vampires can hurt you is if you let them in.

They can’t get in if you tell them no. Following your gut instincts, say no if something they ask of you doesn’t feel right.

5. If you are in contact with vampires, and you can't limit it, make sure you set aside some me-time. This is the time you need to help recharge and regain the energy that those vampires have sucked out of you.

6. Create well-established boundaries that have repercussions when crossed. The only way boundaries work is if something happens to the other person if they don’t respect them. If a coworker is constantly asking you to finish up their work assignments, tell them that you will only be willing to help them if they ask before lunch so that you have time to work on it during work hours. If they don’t, then you don’t do it for them. Chances are, they will just do it themselves or will find some other patsy.

7. Lastly, make a list of your friends and figure out which ones make you feel bad and which ones life you up. Those who make you feel bad should be cut out of your life, or at least cut back the time you spend with them.

The biggest thing I want to make sure that you remember to do is to guard yourself. You don't have to have a victim mindset like everybody is always out to get you, but you do have to make sure that you watch out for yourself. If something just feels off, then speak up and don't let yourself be bullied into that situation.

Healing Exercises

To round out this section, I'm going to provide you with some exercise that can help you heal from the damage that these narcissists and energy vampires have done. They are simple exercises, but they will require self-reflection and stepping outside of your comfort zone.

1. Why are you afraid of expressing yourself?

First, I want you to take some time to write down the reasons why you are afraid to express yourself. This doesn’t mean expressing your feelings, per se, but speaking up. I get it. I’ve been where you are. You hear this person telling you things they want you to do, but all you can think is, “I really don’t want to do that. That doesn’t sound right to me.” But what do you do? Nothing. You go ahead and do it even though it makes you feel bad. I want you to figure out why you do this.

I'll tell you why I didn't like expressing myself, and that was because I would either hurt their feelings, or they would make fun of me. Those are very common excuses for empaths because all we want to do is make people feel happy and be loved, but we can't go through life looking out for everybody else.

2. What boundaries are you not willing to cross in your relationships?

This can be a tough one for a lot of empaths. We’ve had no boundaries for the majority of our life, so coming up with ones can be hard. But that's what you need to do right now. Write out the things that you won't do, and this should be for all of your relationships; romantic, friendships, work, and family. This is especially important if you know the person is a narcissist or an energy vampire.

Boundaries could range from your romantic partner not calling your while you're at work or your coworkers, not asking you for something when you are actively working on something. This can include physical boundaries, as well. Like if you like to relax in your car during a break at work, you could tell a nosy coworker that they are not to knock on your window or disturb you when they see you sitting in your car. When you come up with these, you have to figure out what the consequences are when these boundaries are crossed. I know this task keeps getting harder.

You will have to figure out what the punishment fits the bill. If you're dealing with a busy-body coworker, the punishment could simply be they aren't allowed to talk to you until they are willing to respect your boundaries. The tricky part is, now, you have to let them know about these boundaries. You can't come up with boundaries and not tell them, and then get upset when they cross them. They didn't even know they existed. You have to let them know. Now, the biggie is actually following through with this.

3. What do you want to express in your relationship?

In any relationship that you feel needs to work, and there is a chance for improvement, I want you to make a list of the things that you would like to express about the relationship. This list can be as short or as long as you feel it should be, but typically the longer, the better. Then, I want you to express one of those points each day until you have expressed all of them. Yes, this is going to be hard. Yes, this is going to feel unnatural. But please trust me that this is going to make things better in the long run. If the person you are expressing these points to truly cares, they will listen. Don't worry about scaring them off because if you do, then chances are that it wasn't a healthy relationship to begin with.

4. Who do you want to be?

This one is a bit more fun. All I need you to do is write down the traits that you would like to see in yourself. This could include things like being more assertive, outspoken, confident, strong, and so on. This list can be as long or short as you would like it to be. Really search for yourself when you do this because the purpose of this is to improve yourself. Once you are done, choose a person that you admire who exhibits these same traits. This could be somebody you know personally, or it could be a celebrity of some sort, and then write their name at the top of your list. Now you have a person to look up to that can help you learn how to become those things you want to be.

With this person in mind, it can help you to overcome your fear of expressing yourself. When you start feeling afraid or nervous about speaking up for yourself, telling a person no, or not letting people run over, think about this person. How would they respond to the situation? Take note of how this makes you feel.

Chapter 6: Sex, Drugs, Alcohol, And More

Why do empaths get so addicted to shopping, gambling, food, sex, drugs, alcohol, and other things?

Empaths are extremely prone to behaviors that are addictive since this causes the brain to release dopamine, which is the feel-good hormone.

The main question isn't how addiction happens, but why we are always looking for pleasure? What's more important is what we can do about the addictions, habits, and behaviors we struggle with? An empath's aptitude for feeling everything intensely and understanding what is happening in other people's minds predisposes empaths to addiction and depression.

Empaths feel with other people feel. This can either be good or bad. When things are good, they are great. Empaths will amplify these emotions, and this is why many empaths look for support.

The bad news is that empaths can absorb negative emotions. Emotions are energy that vibrations at various frequencies. Love and joy are high vibrations while shame and guilt and low vibrations.

These vibrations can impact our vitality, quality of life, and mental states.

If empaths don't know ways to efficiently and effectively process all this energy we take in daily, we will either hold it, or we act out. Neither one of these is a healthy way to deal with it. If we hold all this in, it might take on the form of an illness, or it could turn mental. Whichever way, it will get stored either in our brains or our bodies.

We will then have a buildup of toxic emotions in our veins and tissues that are making us feel horrible.

Empaths get overstimulated and overwhelmed because of their oversensitivity. If they begin "feeling too much," and this includes others on their own pain, some empaths will try to self-medicate. If they can't manage the overload to their senses, they will numb their systems to shut down the feelings and thoughts to lessen their empathy even though not everybody knows about this motivation.

They pay an extremely high price for coping with their sensitivities with addictions. The addiction will wear down their spirit, mind, and body and creates anxiety, depression, and illness while trying to manage their over-stimulated world. Addictions just give them a short-term relief from all their overloaded senses, but in the long run, the drugs will stop working and will make the overwhelming feeling much worse.

Evaluating Yourself And Finding Support

Even though not every addict or alcoholic will absorb other's energy, there are many that do. The bad news is that most empaths don't ever get diagnosed and never realize how their high sensitivity and overstimulation fuels their addiction. It is critical to know whether you are coping with your sensitivities engaging in addictive behaviors. How can you figure this out? You need to answer these questions:

- Do you self-medicate to ease the stress or social anxiety you get from others?
- Have you tried to stop using drugs, drinking, or overeating for one month but only last a couple of days, even though you have the best intentions?
- Have you ever thought: "Life would be better if I didn't overeat or drink?"

If you think you are overeating, doing drugs, drinking, or other addictive behaviors to manage your sensory overload, take time to think about how you handle things by looking at the following statements.

You turn to substances when...

1. You want to shut out and escape the world.
2. Energy vampires drain you.

3. You need an energy boost because you feel tired.
4. You stay isolated at home, and you have to have some confidence to go out with others.
5. You don't fit in; you feel anxious and shy.
6. You feel rejected, blamed, or criticized.
7. You feel unsafe emotionally in social situations.
8. You have problems sleeping.
9. You don't feel comfortable in your own skin.
10. Your feelings get hurt easily.
11. You are in emotional pain, feeling depressed, anxious, or frustrated.
12. You get overwhelmed by emotions, whether they are others or your own.

Here is how you can interpret this assessment:

1. If you answered “yes” to just one statement, it shows that you will turn to an addiction to help you handle your sensitivities.

2. If you answered “yes” to between two and five statements, you are moderately using your addiction to help you self-medicate your feelings.

3. If you answered “yes” to six or more statements, you are largely using your addiction to help you deal with your empathy.

Why Empaths Become Addicts

Solicitude is an earnest attention or concern. This is a pretty good description of what empaths feel for the universe, planet, humans, and the world. But it doesn’t describe the sensitivity that is usually associated with an empath. It also doesn’t express the suffering and pain that these people take on. These people can feel specific emotions and energies, both close and far away. Empaths with addictions aren't uncommon.

Once empathy and awareness get overwhelming, empaths will find ways to distract themselves from the discomfort they are feeling. Many people call empaths overly emotional, too sensitive, and some get mislabeled as manic depressive or bipolar. This is understandable since empaths can quickly become sad or emotional depending on the conversation, lights, sounds, and activity around them.

If you are an empath, you know when you pick up extra energy, and you expect some ups and downs. Emotional upset, sudden laughter, sudden crying, and mental confusion are all indicators of an empath on the verge of a breakdown. This could happen anywhere and anytime for empaths. Due to being labeled and all the experience, empaths usually find a temporary escape to stop the sensitivity and will decide to distract themselves with various addictions.

Addictions Empaths Use

If you are an empath, you can't just flip a switch and turn off the world and emotions. To escape all the energy, many will partake in activities that could do more harm than good.

1. Exercise

Nothing will get endorphins flowing like a workout. This addiction is sort of healthy. Moderate exercise is a great distraction, but if you take this to extremes, it could cause too much weight loss or injuries. Many empaths will get consumed with exercising to keep their minds distracted from all the emotions they feel.

2. Solitude

This is actually one addiction that I love. Shutting out everything and being alone. If I leave home, answer my phone, or scroll through social media, I will become burdened. I love spending my days in solitude.

3. Drama

Most empaths seem to be addicted to any and all drama that unfolds in their energy field. It might seem odd to try to drown out all the emotionally overwhelming situations with even more drama, but many people say it is a way for them to redirect their energy.

4. Alcohol and Drugs

Most empaths will partake in spirits to try and lift theirs. Others will go for prescription sedatives. Some will even try to tune into other worlds by using psychedelics or marijuana. Yes, these are going to give you some relief, but using alcohol or drugs daily can have adverse effects on a person's spiritual, emotional, and physical well-being with time.

Alternatives For Addictions

If you are an empath and have been using your addiction as a distraction or to get rid of emotional or physical woes that come with that gift, you should know that there are other ways:

1. Aura Shielding

You can create a grid around your aura and yourself when you don't want to receive anybody else's energy.

2. Be Open

Rather than blocking and numbing, you need to become open and then surrender to your gift of being an empath.

3. Food

You can raise your vibrations by eating healthy foods. Foods that have high vibrations could improve your strength and boost your mood to help battle all those lows and highs.

4. Herbs

Most herbs and herbal teas will help calm you.

5. Go Outside

Find a spot in nature that you feel at one with and soak up some wonderful energy.

6. Meditation

You can help calm yourself with some good old-fashioned meditation instead of medication. Practicing meditation will help you breathe in calmness and breathe out all the negative emotions that you have absorbed.

7. Crystals and Stones

Carrying or wearing crystals can help shield your aura and alleviate stress. Calming stones include amethyst, blue lace agate, black tourmaline, shungite, rose quartz, and lepidolite. You could use crystal grids to help protect your energy.

Solutions And Strategies

Being self-aware can be liberating. There isn't any shame about it. No need to blame anyone. Once you are aware of your addiction, you will be gaining an appreciation of how to handle your empathy. You will then be able to deal with the addiction more productively. Here are some steps to help you manage addition:

1. Identify the Addiction

You have to honestly assess the amount you take substances or drink each week. How many times do you overeat to handle feeling overwhelmed? Have you participated in any other addictions like excessive work, internet, video games, shopping, gambling, love, or sex to lower your anxiety? Learn to be compassionate with yourself. Find patterns where you self-medicate your feelings. If you self-medicate just one time a week or a month shows that you might have a problem with addiction.

2. Nothing Will Help

You have to understand that nothing in the world: no money, job, person, or substance will ever make you feel comfortable with your sensitivities or yourself. You only find happiness on the inside. You have to learn to accept, love and know yourself. This takes a complete lifetime. The more you try to run away from your sensitivities, you will become more uncomfortable. To quote Buddha: "There is no external refuge."

3. Therapy

You should have an ongoing plan to help you with your addiction. You could look into 12-step programs or psychotherapy. You have to find ones that inspire you to have a healthy relationship with others and yourself. Since you are an empath, you won't be relying on drugs to hand the sensory overload or painful feelings. You will be able to find balance and to center your life.

Here are some things you can do to help:

1. Rest

Get out of your routine on a regular basis. You need to have two very distinct environments, one that is our normal everyday lives and one where we can go and recharge. If we don't have these two environments, everything will begin to blend together, and we won't very completely disconnect, and we won't be doing our best when we are at work. We are going to stay in between where we are dissatisfied and looking for something that makes us feel better.

2. Release

Are you holding onto things? Are there stories or emotions you need to let go of? If you have energy stored from your entire life, you need to begin with this step. This release isn't going to happen at one time. It could, with some practice of being aware of your body's signals and letting go. We have a horrible habit of hanging on to things we don't think we can handle. If there is pain from something that happened when you were a child, you are holding it because you don't believe you are strong enough to deal with it. Let me tell you right now that you do. You are stronger than you think. You may just need to find the right kind of support.

3. Restore

Anywhere there is suffering, there will be a lack of integrity. We aren't talking about a state of being whole. Part of being human is we are born with wounds in our souls. We have a job of reintegrating and healing all the perceived parts of ourselves that are "unlovable" so we can be connected with each other. All the parts of you that you have cast off are the reason you are suffering. Everyone in the world is trying to cope with this disease. Empaths feel powerlessness and pain.

4. Manage

You have to learn to manage your energy, time, and emotions. You might not feel like you have the energy or time, so you go to what is convenient and easy. Managing emotions will free up some energy that you have been spending on things that will never serve you. You get messages from your emotions. These alert you to any boundaries that someone might have crossed. Think about your boundaries. Are any of them being crossed? Do you even have boundaries? Not knowing and enforcing your boundaries will cause you more stress, frustration, and work than you are able to manage. This makes you want to sit in front of the television with a whole pizza and a bottle of wine. This will make you lonely, broke, sick, and overweight.

5. Manifest

You have to use your gift. Be active. Be organized. Be confident. Be connected. Be clear. You will see the results. Addictions are very distracting. They are very disruptive and can totally destroy your life. Empaths won't ever be average, so you need to quit trying to act normal. You were born with an awesome gift. You have to learn to use it. Once you have learned to use it, your life will light up. You need to figure out what your gift is if you don't know. You will be missing out on the best that life has for you if you don't find out your gift. You will probably fall into just coping with feeling like a failure and being completely misunderstood. You need to try everything in your power to not let this happen. If you aren’t already there, don't worry, there is a cure.

6. Move

Get moving. Move your body. Exercise does wonders for the mind and body. Most empaths will look for comfort in their own inner world. This is where they feel loved and safe. The problem happens when they are stuck there for way too long. Staying isolated will lead to addiction. They try to cope with loneliness and stress by using behaviors and substances that trigger dopamine as a way to avoid self-awareness and painful emotions. If we commit to living a life where we move our bodies and get the dopamine flowing and reconnecting to the things we enjoy, such as our families and friends, we will be flying higher than any drug, alcohol, or food can ever take us.

To Sum It Up

There are both environmental and biological factors behind addictions. Humans are programmed to want pleasure. Our brains get hit with dopamine the same way no matter whether the fix is nicotine, caffeine, heroin, cocaine, or sugar. It might be a behavior like looking at our phones, watching television, gambling, or shopping.

Empaths are more prone to addiction since we are so sensitive to the feelings of others and our own. We can feel all the powerlessness, anxiety, and feat that is in the world. Because of all the pain, not being able to process it, we "cope" with behaviors that make us "feel good," and we get addicted. We will try to fix it since we feel broken. We usually find that normal therapies won't work. Try all the things listed above, and please seek help before it's too late.

Chapter 7: How Empathic Children Can Blossom Into Young Adults

You have to be able to recognize that your child is an empath, so you can support them if you want them to grow up happy and able to use their gift to the best of their ability.

Empathy isn't an easy gift, and if you grew up as an empath, you probably remember getting called emotional, over-sensitive, and needy. If we don't get understood as children, it affects us psychologically as we grow up. This is why we absolutely have to recognize empathy in our children and give them the support and love they need to love their gift instead of resenting it.

Empathic children need our support to help them deal with emotions that feel overwhelming to them. It is easy for us to make them feel horrible instead of better if we don't treat them sensitively.

Each child is a person, but if your child shows these signs, they are probably an empath:

1. Reacts Badly to Specific Situations or People

If you aren't an empath, you could become embarrassed if your child isn't nice to a family member or a close friend. It could be that your child is absorbing energy that you aren't aware of. You shouldn't ever force your child to be with people they are afraid of, or they don't like.

You have to trust your child on this one. If you are in an abusive or negative relationship, then you have to do something about it for your sake but for the sake of your child who might find it very damaging.

Take your children's fears of heart. They might not always be able to tell you when a situation or person makes them feel uncomfortable since they are afraid of upsetting you. You will see it through the way they behave. They might become unhappy, withdrawn, or show some physical symptoms like feeling sick or having tummy aches. Talk to them when they are unhappy to try to get to the root of the problem.

2. Physical Symptoms

Most children who are empaths will suffer from stomach aches, headaches, sore throats, or other physical ailments. You might have taken them to the doctor for the doctor to tell you that they can't find anything wrong with them. This doesn't mean that their pain isn't real. This is the only way they know to ask for help and express all the feelings they have inside.

Being upset and anxious can settle in the stomach, causing a lot of discomforts. Frustrations and tension cause headaches. If your child has strep, tonsillitis, and sore throats a lot, they are experiencing a lot of emotional problems.

Science has shown that emotional stress can manifest itself as endocrine disruption, inflammation, and physical pain. Don't ever dismiss their physical symptoms. Instead, show them support and sympathy. They are only looking for reassurance and comfort. Giving them a hug and talking with them will make their symptoms go away.

If they feel as if they aren't being listened to or if they have problems talking about what they are going through, make some homemade popsicles and help them express their feelings by letting them draw or write until they can talk to you about it.

If they have a lot of stomach problems, try giving them some ginger ale or peppermint tea. These will help soothe the tummy. You could also try some gentle yoga or some deep breathing.

When you have them calmed down, see if you can help them find where the upset is coming from and find some solutions together.

3. Sensitive to Emotions

Empathic children often pick up on all the emotions around them. Never think you can hide your feelings when you are worried or angry. They know. Just because you don't fight in front of them, they still can feel the tension. Empathic children will be able to pick up on the atmosphere, energy, and body language. They can feel the emotions of others, and this is very distressing for them, too.

Try to be open with your child no matter how old they are. It won't be worth trying to hide any problem from them. They are going to know that some are wrong and that you are trying to hide it from them. This makes them fear the worst. They could also begin blaming themselves. It is better to talk with them about all the problems and reassure them that you have it handled, and they shouldn't worry about it.

4. They "Don't Belong."

Every empath I've encountered doesn't feel like they belong on this planet, and this feeling usually begins during early childhood. Children who are empaths will experience the world a lot different than all the other kids, and this can cause empathic children to feel alienated.

Your child may not know how to play right with others, or they get overwhelmed by boisterous playing or the rules of the game. What's "in" might not be of interest to them, and they get ostracized by other children.

You can tell your child they are special, but it isn't going to make them feel any better. You are still going to feel resentful and will feel like the only person that accepts them is you.

Never tell them to “try harder” to be what they aren’t. This will only crush their spirits and could manifest in them becoming depressed or extremely anxious.

Help them find their “people” as early as possible. If they have certain interests, look for groups where there are children the same age, so they will be able to socialize with others.

If your child is older, let them join online groups or go to camps that focus on their interests. When they can spend time with children who are similar to them, they won't feel as lonely. They might not fit with one group, but they will know there are others that will appreciate and accept them.

5. They Are Musical or Artistic

Just like some empaths are drawn to nature, there are some drawn to music and art, either enjoying or creating it. If your child has problems expressing themselves talking, they might find it easier to paint or draw. They could also enjoy looking at colorful paintings or comic books. If they have anxiety, they might feel better working with clay. Various types of music could help soothe them, and it could inspire them to play an instrument.

You need to encourage them without judging and whenever you can. If your child shows you an abstract painting, never try to interpret it, just ask them to tell you about it. You can say something like: "I really love how you used the color purple here. Can you tell me how you felt when you painted this?"

Or you could say: "This painting looks like it will tell a story. Can you help me understand it so I can appreciate it?"

If your child shows interest in learning to play an instrument, work with them to find one that they are interested in but one that won't drive you crazy. A cello or violin might cost more than a recorder, but it won't be as annoying.

6. Vivid Dreams

The lucid, vivid dreams that most empaths have usually begun when they were very young. These dreams might be extremely intense. They might have clairsentient, clairvoyant aspects, or they might be night terrors. It doesn't matter whether the dreams are terrifying or wonderful; they could have a strong effect on an empathic child.

Help your child start a dream journal to help them process all the things they saw. They can read back over it from time to time and see what images or dreams have recurred. Most empaths will be clairvoyant or claircognizant, and sometime these dreams will come true. All of this usually starts during childhood and could either be scary or intriguing to a child.

You could help them keep a journal by recording your dreams along with them and look back over them if the dreams were to come true. If the dream does come true, reassure your child that there isn't anything wrong with them. They just possess a wonderful, beautiful gift. Always remember to use positive reinforcement all the time.

7. Alone Time

Just as adult empaths need and crave alone time, so does the child empath. They normally don't ever get bored, since, well, how can they? Most of these don't like being alone; they NEED that time for many reasons. If your child has had a meltdown due to sensory overload, some quiet, alone time is just what the doctor ordered. Think about it like this;

our skin needs time to heal after a cut or burn; their souls need time to heal after an overload.

Never, ever reprimand your child for wanting to be alone or demand they engage with others. You will never be able to get blood out of a stone. As adults, we have days that we feel completely drained after working all day, and we have a strong desire for solitude and silence and want our wishes respected.

Children are at our mercy, and they feel as if they have to give in to our demands for social interaction or be ready for punishment. Please, above all, you do, respect their need for solitude, and recognize that it doesn't have anything to do with you, and there isn't anything "wrong" with your child. They aren't rejecting you, and it isn't unhealthy for them needing alone time rather than playing with others. Your child will appreciate you more for allowing them some alone time.

8. Information Sponges

Does your child get interested in everything? Do they get fascinated by a certain topic and then need to learn all there is to learn about it? This is a common trait for empaths, and it normally begins as soon as they can hold their heads up. They think everything is fascinating and miraculous, and they have so much to learn. Your child might have begun reading at a young age, and they demand frequent visits to the library where they can read everything they can find on whatever has their attention on this day. If your child has a disability, they might like history documentaries or being in nature.

You have to encourage this behavior every time you can. If the topics they like don't interest you, this is fine, just be honest with them. Encourage them to explore these topics by themselves or other people who have similar interests.

9. Nature Lover

Nature is very healing for empaths for many reasons, so you have to understand that this goes double for children. Children are drawn to nature, and they love exploring it. There is a lot to smell and see when in nature. Being in nature is very calming, and anyone can benefit from getting some exercise in the sunshine and fresh air. If a child spends a lot of time outside, they are usually drawn to gardening, animal rights activism, and environmental stewardship. They will love growing things, observing animals in their natural habitats, and nurturing life. Children who are empaths get recharged by playing in the soil, water, or sitting with their backs against trees.

Try to get your child out in nature regularly. If you are lucky and have a backyard, help them create an herb or vegetable garden for themselves. Plant flowers that will attract birds and butterflies, and place shallow bowls of water for toads and frogs. If you live in an apartment, find local parks or community gardens where you can take your child. Leave the city and go camping or on hikes when you can. Get involved in things your child is interested in. Do they love to look at the stars? Get a telescope and learn the constellations with them. Are they healers? Take an herbal medicine course and go foraging for plants.

10. They Become Upset by Unpleasant Television or Movies

Everyone has experienced moments when watching a movie or television when we have had to look away from something that is very unpleasant. For many, this is fleeting, and we can just dismiss it. For small empathic children, this doesn't happen. They will empathize with the characters so deeply that an unpleasant scene will upset them terribly. If it is too traumatic, it could cause depression, nightmares, or even haunt them for many years.

If you know what triggers your child, do some research before you watch a television show or film with them to see if there will be anything that will upset them. Most children will be very upset if an animal gets hurt, so stay away from movies like this. Empathic children will need to create some coping mechanism with time, so they won't have to hide away forever. It is good to expose them to some unpleasant imagery a little at a time if you feel they can handle it. You can begin with cartoons because it is easier for them to understand that these are make-believe, and nobody gets hurt. Learning how much suffering is happening in the world could be very overwhelming for these little people. Gentleness is the order of the day and for as long as it is possible.

11. Compassion for Objects that Aren't Alive

If your child gets upset if you throw away a broken bowl because they think the bowl will feel abandoned and hurt, chances are they are an empath. Children who empathize with others sometimes have problems with anthropomorphism. They don't realize that their stuffed animals don't have nerves as we do, and they don't feel pain if it gets a boo-boo.

If the child is under the age of four, put a bandage on the animal's boo-boo. Apologize to the broken bowl for sending it back home to get fixed. Older kids could be comforted in animistic rituals where their spirit gets thanked and honored for all the joy it brought your child. Encourage your child to set the items spirit free before they recycle it. Don't use phrases such as tossed out or thrown away, and these can indicate abandonment. Show them how everything will gain a new purpose in life, even when transformed into new shapes.

12. They Think A Lot

Children who are empaths are the ones who teachers will tell they spend too much time "in their heads." They even get accused of daydreaming and are told to stop being so serious and to lighten up. These young children are analyzing each aspect of existence and trying to make sense of the world while reveling in all the wonders it gives. They are trying to understand sarcasm, duplicity, and other contradictory behaviors.

You need to ask them what they might be thinking about. If they choose to tell you, use active listening. Show true interest in their thoughts, ask them challenging questions that are appropriate for their age, and validate their thoughts. When you encourage your child with this deep thinking, it could help them move into careers where they can use their analytical and intellectual nature.

13. Connects With Animals

It is always easier for empaths to connect with friends who aren't human. Animal behaviors make sense to the empath. They aren't filled with conflicting verbal expressions and body language. Animal friends accept humans without questions, they don't judge, or aren't cruel like human children could be.

You have to encourage their behavior. Be sure your child has an animal to take care of and spend time with. Just make sure that you do any allergy testing on other family members before you get a pet. There isn't anything more devastating to an empathic child than boding with a pet only to have it ripped from their arms and heart just because somebody else has allergies.

14. Deep Feelings

Children who are empaths usually feel things a lot deeper than another will. Where one child may shrug off getting scolded and go back to playing in a few minutes, empathic children might be completely devastated. They will hurt deeply after they are reprimanded, but they will feel terrible about disappointing their parents. They will also feel embarrassed about being scolded in front of their friends, along with shame and guilt about not controlling their emotions. These children have to deal with their emotions like a layer cake constantly. They are aware of what everybody else is feeling, and this magnifies their own responses. Whatever they feel at any moment, they will feel it more intensely than other children will. This holds true for happiness, too.

Never invalidate their feelings and NEVER make fun of them for how they respond. If a child is teased or mocked when they dance or bounce in delight, they might learn that they can't express their joy. The same thing goes for sorrow.

Chapter 8: A Powerful Recovery Strategy For Empaths In Trouble

If you are an empath, you know you feel deeply for others. You don't feel sorry for them; you feel the actual emotional pain that somebody else is feeling. You don't even have to put any effort toward this either. It is almost like a sixth sense—having to walk through this world, feeling the pain of others could be overwhelming. Coping with and making sense of somebody's pain is hard to bear, so automatically feeling other's anguish is even more difficult.

Your empathy can be looked at as both a curse and a gift. You easily understand and connect with others. You might find yourself excelling in subjects such as psychology and English. You might feel yourself being pulled into professions like psychotherapy. This means that you get to help others heal for a living. Your job will be to interpret and understand other's experiences and emotions. Having empathy will allow you to help others heal.

When you sit down after working all day and turn on the news, you feel instantly devastated. You feel anxious, discouraged, and completely zapped of energy.

If you can learn to help others heal by using your empathy, you will be able to change the world. When empaths experience empathy for other people, but they can't help them, they get overcome with anxiety and grief. They won't be able to be productive or happy for a few hours.

You need to discriminate when you're an empath. You have to be careful when you get involved with dehumanizing material. Make sure you are able to help others and heal.

If your child is an empath, don't expose them to things that dehumanize others. Stay away from news, movies, or anything that has a lot of graphic content. Ask them if they have any questions about what is happening around them. And answer their questions as thoughtfully and as honestly to the best of your ability. Helping them filter and digest any dehumanizing and graphic material will help protect them.

When your child is upset, listen to them. Never tell them that "they are too sensitive." You could say something like: "You are hurt for your friend. I understand that. You care. This makes you a very good person."

If you are an adult, be sure you have someone you can talk to. Let them help you work through your feelings. This is what loved ones and friends do.

Empaths aren't weak, enablers, or bleeding hearts. Enablers or sympathizers don't feel anyone else's pain. They will actually try to avoid discomfort by helping in other ways. They normally stay detached emotionally. Sometimes you might have to detach if you are interacting with someone who has a personality disorder. If you are a parent and detach yourself from your child, it makes you look like you are emotionally distant or are self-centered.

A parent who enables would call their child's coach to demand the coach change their mind if the coach took the child out of the game. This will give the child a victim mentality.

A parent who is empathetic will go to where their child is emotional. They will let themselves feel the child's hurt so they can understand the child better. They will be able to empathize. They will say something like: "You are disappointed. I understand. I would be disappointed, too. Just keep working hard during practice, and things might change." The child will feel understood because you were empathetic with them. They will feel closer and bonded to you.

Empathy can change a child's brain by creating a good tone in their vagus nerve. This helps to soothe their body and mind. It will create resilience, security, and calmness that will translate into a good work ethic. On the other hand, sympathy will only create a sense of entitlement in a child.

Empathy requires deep emotions that most people don't have. Deep emotions usually go together with selflessness and courage. If an empath is put in a position to heal, they could be the strongest, bravest people around.

Calm Your Nervous System

Because empaths pick up other people's emotions, they are susceptible to anxiety, stress, and depression. Empathy is a wonderful gift, but it does have a shadow side. If you are an empath, you have to learn ways to calm your anxiety to help you stay balanced and healthy.

It is very easy for an empath to get stuck in a state of alarm, panic, and are very overwhelmed. Every empath is born with a very sensitive nervous system. They are always very attuned to all the energy that is around them. Their energy gets easily depleted by narcissistic people, energy vampires, and people who are just addicted to complaining. Being around these people is why empaths develop neurological problems and pain disorders like fibromyalgia.

When we get stressed, there are three stages that our bodies go through.

1. Alarm Stage

This is when our nervous system goes into the flight or fight mode. This is when a stressor gets triggered either psychologically or physically. This can happen if we receive an alarming letter, you've just been in an accident, or you see a snake or spider. Our bodies will produce large amounts of adrenaline to mobilize energy and blood to the major organs and our muscles.

The first step to get out of this stage is to start being aware of the people you are around daily. You need to find out which ones are energy vampires. This is easy to do. All you have to do is take note of who you are around when you begin to feel completely drained. This might be a relationship where there is only one-way intimacy where your partner is constantly taking, and if you ever need anything, you know you can't ask them. This is a great indicator that you need to set stronger boundaries with this person, and we will get into that more in a bit.

If the stressor is ongoing and doesn't stop, the nervous system will go into the next stage:

2. Resistance Stage

In this stage, we get into a negative cycle of trying to cope with the stress. Our bodies will go into an inflammatory stage where it begins to produce more cortisol, which is an anti-inflammatory hormone that is produced by the adrenal gland. It has many negative effects on the body if it gets produced for a long time. One of these negative effects is protein catabolism will begin to break down muscle. We begin to produce less serotonin from the protein that we consume. Our bodies start to have digestive problems. If the stressor stays chronic and doesn't get turned off, our nervous system won't have any choice but to go into the next stage:

3. Exhaustion Stage

This is essentially when our bodies go into burnout. In this stage, our bodies no longer have the ability to adapt, and we begin feeling no motivation, listless, and cynical. Then we are going to need sedative support because even though we are completely exhausted, we won't be able to sleep.

The best way to combat these stages is to nourish your body the right way. You need to reduce the amount of caffeine you drink daily. Have protein-rich food with every meal to help nourish the body and to put less pressure on the adrenal glands. Make sure that you are well hydrated with pure water. Bottled water won't work because it has been filtered the wrong way. Drinking mineral water would be ideal. You need to get plenty of sleep. You can take a magnesium supplement to help you sleep if you would like to. If you have other medical problems, you can always check with your doctor to see if a magnesium supplement is okay for you to take. You can also do grounding techniques, and we will go into this later on. Basically, to ground yourself, you just need to get out in nature. Walking barefoot is the best way to ground. Doing yoga is a great way to recharge; just be careful not to overdo it since your adrenaline glands are already working overtime.

Here are some techniques that will help you stay emotionally balanced and calm your anxiety.

1. Find Yourself

Empaths have a hard time figuring out which emotions belong to others and themselves. This is what causes empaths to feel anxious and never knowing why. To be able to untangle your emotions, feelings, and thoughts from other people's, you have to know your inner self. You could try:

- Be by yourself. You need to take some time for yourself, so you can enjoy things you like without worrying about other people's feelings.

- Working on creative projects like gardening, cooking, or art will help you tune out your thoughts and allows you to express your creativity.
- Writing in a journal about your feelings and thoughts daily.

It is very important to spend time pursuing your dreams and goals and do all the things that you want to do. You will feel like helping others when you are restored and rested. You will feel like you are living with a purpose.

2. Balanced Nervous System

Empaths will always have their channels open. They constantly pick up on the pain and anxiety of others. If you spend a lot of time listening to other people's complaints and fears, it could push your nervous system into overdrive.

Being anxious and stressed could cause health problems like autoimmune diseases and high blood pressure. You could alleviate your anxiety by doing some techniques to calm your nervous system. They could include:

- Learning some emotional shielding techniques to help protect yourself by keeping other people's emotions away from yours.

- Use essential oil like bergamot, chamomile, or lavender. These can be put into a bath, used during a massage, or in a diffuser.

- Take some time for a mindfulness routine or meditation to help calm your nerves.

You need to be aware of your nervous system so you can help yourself move away from the fight or flight mode and stay calm when you are facing hard situations.

3. Know Your Body

Other people's emotions affect empaths physically and emotionally. If you pick up the emotions of others, these could cause you sensations that are uncomfortable like pain, aches, fatigue, and headaches.

Because of this, it is vital that you look after your physical self. You could begin with some grounding techniques that will help you feel comfortable with your own body. You could try:

- Massaging your shoulders, feet, or hands or getting a full body massage.
- Spend time in nature to recharge and ground yourself. Being barefoot would be best.
- Creating a simple yoga routine to the ground and destress yourself.

Empaths spend a lot of time in their own heads. Being more aware of how their body feels could give a completely new perspective on life and their interactions with others. You have to listen to your body as this is vital to your wellbeing and good health.

4. Creating Boundaries

Empaths are natural-born givers. Because you experience the emotions of others, you always want to help others. You want to ease the pain of others since this will ease your pain, too. When you always put other people first, it isn't a healthy way to live. This is why empaths experience anxiety, stress, and depression.

Creating boundaries is essential to keep an empaths' emotions balanced. Each empath is different, just like all humans are different. Your boundaries will be different from other empaths' boundaries. You have to take time to think about the things that will help you feel better.

If you constantly get stressed out, burned out, and anxious, you won't be able to help others, so you have to put your needs first. This isn't being selfish. It is being sensible. You might want to introduce some things that will help you keep your emotional balance. These could include:

- Take time for things that are important to you.
- Limit the time you spend around people who drain you emotionally.
- Schedule quiet time for yourself daily to recharge.

You have to make all these things a priority. You have every right to live your life the way you want to and not to give your energy to others. When you can do this, you will notice that your anxiety has lessened, and you will feel happier.

Stop Being A People Pleaser

Empaths will betray themselves in little ways. They agree when they actually don't. They listen when they are completely drained of energy. They will stop what they are doing to do something for someone else.

Pleasing others is an unconscious, common impulse for empaths. This happens because they feel that other people are upset with them in their hearts; they know other's discomfort very intimately. Empaths have huge hearts. They are givers. They are lovers. And they put themselves last.

This won't serve their relationships or themselves. They love being kind. They love to make other people happy. But all this comes at a cost. They are sacrificing themselves.

They want other people's discomfort and pain to disappear. They never want to disappoint others. They unwittingly think they can make others happy.

People-pleasing is a pattern that gets ingrained deeply that begins at a very young age. They learned to suppress their desires and needs. They oriented to the things that other people needed and completely lost what feels right for them.

This pattern could begin from being mistreated or having low self-worth. They believe if they sacrifice for other people, they will be treated better. They will finally get everything they haven't ever gotten, whether it is acceptance, attention, or love.

When you leave your needs out of a relationship, it won't ever work. Healthy relationships take two people who are authentic and actually show up. If not, then resentment will begin building up. They will either act passive-aggressively or withdraw completely.

To end this people-pleasing, an empath has to learn to PAUSE before they respond. Figure out what feels right at this moment. Do YOU need anything? What will work for YOU? You have to learn to directly and clearly state your needs, disagree, or just say "NO."

The first step in stopping an empath from being a people pleaser is finding the reason behind their need to please. Most of the time, an empath will have two fears. The first fear is the fear of being unloved. The empath has a fear of not being worthy and feeling inconsequential. Due to this underlying fear, the empath will become very adept at scanning their environment, looking for needs in others, and reaching out into the world usually very assertively. Some empaths will reach out in a militant way to make sure a person's needs get met.

When empaths begin to reflect on this, they will see that there is a payoff for them. They get a feeling of exhilaration, connection, and joy. They get a boost to their sense of self because the fear of being unloved motivated their need to please.

What starts happening is their need to please begins to perpetuate this underlying fear that if they aren't helping, pleasing, giving, or reaching out into the world, they aren't worthy or loveable.

What you have to understand is that as an empath, you give because you have worth, and your giving is a manifestation of your innate worth. Instead, many are thinking they gain worth when they give. Empaths need to make this very important distinction.

The next fear is the fear of being without protection. It's a fear of being vulnerable. This fear is different. It has a different flavor and energy. This fear of being without protection makes the empath think that if they don't give or please, if they aren't agreeable and don't go along with what they want, they will view you as a threat. Or they might take away their support and protection.

They both seem to look like they want to give, and please, but the internal motivation is different. In fear of being without protection, there is a lot of anxiety underneath the empath' mask. They might begin fearing retribution or that they are going to be blamed if things don't go the right way. The cause of fear here is that they will lose their security. They will get blamed, so they are going to go along to get along.

If you are in a relationship with a person who has a predatory personality like somebody who has a narcissistic personality disorder, the narcissist will trigger both of these fears for the empath. Triggering both of these fears will put the empath in a very precarious position where they end up going into a hyper activate mode of needing to please, and this causes the nervous system to go completely haywire.

You have to figure out what the motivation is for these underlying fears before you can begin to use strategies to stop them. For fear of being unloved, the best thing an empath can do is to increase their insight and to increase their awareness. Then they can begin actively taking steps to stop reaching out to others. For fear of being without protection, the empath needs to reclaim their own sense of authority, internal capacity, and find resources they can use to deal with the world and authority figures.

They have to realize that they possess a reservoir of experiences, and they have an internal warrior that can and will protect them. They don't have to sell themselves just to be agreeable in exchange for some bad protection. Empaths can use any strategy that helps with assertion, any strategy that helps gain a sense of authority, and a sense of being grounded in their own authority.

This habit of being a people pleaser will change, but it is very slow. Your relationships will start being reciprocal. You will begin getting as much as you give. You will find that you are able to still be kind without sacrificing yourself. You will have relationships that are fulfilling for yourself and your partner.

Be Gentle With Yourself

Everybody has an internal critic or judge. We have to learn how to quiet this part of us so we can learn how to be gentler on ourselves. The internal critic is the part of us that is the repository of the critical messages, the put-downs, the wounds that we have accumulated over our lifetime.

This internal critic is masterful at triggering the hypercritical messages and wounds. The internal critic gets inflated in everyone who is under stress. Stress can come from physical or psychological stressors. Basically, any situation that makes us use our resources. If that stress becomes chronic and unrelenting and our resources get compromised to the point that our bodies can't meet our demands, this is when we find that the critical messages of the internal critic will become more active.

Narcissistic people are experts at triggering the empaths' internal critic because the narcissist is able to use the empaths' vulnerabilities against them. This is an area where narcissists use the vulnerabilities of others in order to fake empathy, to fake concern for others, and to manipulate them.

There are some things you need to understand about the internal critic. This internal critic operates like a hologram. When the internal critic is activated, we no longer see it for what it really is. This "hologram" doesn't have any power over us. Still, when we are under a lot of stress, then this internal critic becomes inflated to the point that it is experienced as three dimensional or being real. An empath who has an inflated judge will become more unaware and more unable to disconnect themselves from the messages of the judge.

The judge could lay dormant, and under conditions of incredible stress, it will pop up. When the judge is going full throttle at us when our internal judge is attacking us, it disables our higher reasoning centers. The judge works at our subcortical level, where it is able to cause us to feel angry, rage, panic, and fear. We have to realize that this judge works best when we are under a lot of stress.

When our bodies are under chronic, unrelenting stress, it can deplete our bodies of minerals like potassium and magnesium. Some of the symptoms of being a judge dominated personality, and these don't just apply to empaths, so a narcissistic person can be very judge dominated as well. We can see this in their need for control and power domination. Their internal critic has dominated people who have victim-mentality, chronic complaining, cynicism, and resentment.

There are ways to shrink the internal critic, but you have to understand that you can't get rid of the internal critic totally. You just need to learn to be aware of when your internal critic goes from being dormant to become activated. When predatory people, manipulative people, narcissistic people trigger our internal critic by making us feel guilty, making us second guess ourselves. We need to have an awareness that there has been a shift inside us and that we have lost touch with our internal authority.

A very important part of dealing with our internal critic is for us to work on strengthening our inner observer so you can start to identify your internal critic's signature. What are the signature signs that our internal critic has been triggered? This will usually be certain themes that we will begin to experience about ourselves. Themes of failure, I'm not good enough, I'm a bad person, I've made a mistake, or things aren't going to work out for me. These are all typical themes of critical messages that the judge will trigger within the empath.

Becoming aware that it isn't really about a certain situation and that the internal critic isn't sophisticated; it is lurking in the background just waiting for us to experience some stress, to feel compromised, and then it will attack. It will attack you with a familiar theme. When you are stressed, the inflation of the internal critic makes it harder for you to see that the internal critic isn't real.

In order to overcome the internal critic, you can do anything that will calm the nervous system. Do something that will take you out of the sympathetic nervous system activation and into the parasympathetic nervous system. What I mean to say is, basically, rest and digest will help shrink the judge.

Another good way of dealing with your internal critic is to identify the energy vampires that are in your life. These people excel at triggering your stress levels: the internal critic, the narcissist, the chronic complainer, and the dramatic people where drama always seems to surround them. When you are around these types of people, you need to strengthen your inner observer and be extremely aware of any subtle shifts in how you start to experience yourself and the internal messages that you are starting to have about yourself.

You have to understand that stress of any kind—even if it doesn't have to do with a narcissistic person—is difficult. You might just be stuck in traffic, or you're late for work, and you can't find your keys. These situations can inflate the internal critic.

Support Group

Some empaths get so bogged down with other people's energy that they forget who they are and how to survive. If you have tried all the above suggestions and they don't seem to work for you, you can try to find a support group. Support groups allow you to talk about everything that is bothering you. They might be able to give you some insight into how to handle your problems. There are several different types of support groups. If you aren't comfortable talking in person to others, you might look online for support groups. You can find all sorts of support groups on Facebook or meetup. Some churches will have counselors that hold various meetings for people where they help people open up about their problems. Call your local hospitals or community services to see if they can help you find one in your area. Talking with others is a great way to heal yourself. Never feel less of a person if you have to ask for help. You can and will get through this.

Chapter 9: Healing The Spirit-Mind Connection

Once you realize that you are an empath, you have to create and be extremely strict with boundaries. These are the most helpful and needed protection tools.

Empaths have big hearts and like helping others. You need to be able to tell the difference between whether or not you are helping others, and if you are just wasting energy that hasn't been replenished yet. You have to be aware of energy vampires since they get drawn to empaths. You might notice that you feel drained when you spend time with a certain person. You need to look closely at this relationship as it might be doing you more harm than good.

Empaths have wonderful strengths that need to be developed. These are things like depth, intuition, compassion, and connecting to the Earth along with other people. The World could use your gifts, and this is why you need to get in touch with your Warrior Spirit.

Empaths who have the following strategic, energy-saving tools can't be stopped. Here are some strategies that I used to support my Warrior Spirit. Try them out and see if your clarity and energy improve. You don't have to use them all. Pick and choose and do what works best for you.

Here are some tools that you could use:

- Develop and Use Energy Shields

This is more of a spiritual tool, but it is one that you can take with you wherever you go.

You can't avoid every stressful situation and everybody who drains your energy. Every now and then, you might have to sit beside an energy vampire, or you might have to go to an event or place that is very emotional such as visiting a person who is sick and in the hospital. These types of situations are going to drain you. If you can develop and use an energy shield for protection, you will be able to handle anything that life throws at you.

This is a spiritual and mental barrier that you visualize encircles you. It is a bubble of light where anything negative will never get through. Once you have developed this ability, put it in practice daily, and you will soon be strong enough to handle every situation.

- Be a Great Communicator

Since empaths feel like they are connected to other people, romantic relationships can be difficult because empaths need alone time, and their significant others don't understand this. This is where great communication comes into play.

Being able to communicate well is a protection tool if you can learn to use it as one. If you can learn to express all the things you feel, this will open up a world of possibilities. You might have to ask your significant other for breaks during the day if you are with each other all day. You are going to need more physical space, such as a larger bed or a meditation room for yourself.

- Have Protective Stones with You

You can use crystals to help keep you grounded. Many gemstones have great connections to Mother Earth, which helps keep you grounded. Since you are very sensitive to energy, you might have realized that when you get near certain crystals, they hold a charge similar to a battery. When you sleep near, wear, or carry one, it can help you recalibrate and restore your energy. It works best if you pick a crystal that you resonate with. There are many crystals that you could use, but clear quartz, fluorite, kunzite, rose quartz, amethyst, spirit quartz, aventurine, and tourmaline are the best. Remember to cleanse them regularly either under running water, pass them through some burning sage, place them out in the sun, or bury them in some sea salt for a few minutes. If you cleanse them underwater, make sure they are able to be used in water.

- Spend Time in Nature

If you have had a difficult day, you can restore your energy by getting out in nature. You need to do this by yourself. You can combine your much needed “me time” with nature.

Empaths tend to feel a connection to nature, especially animals and trees. If you suddenly get an urge to sit outside and watch the birds or squirrels play or even hug a tree, these acts might seem small, but they can recharge your energy quickly.

The most important thing to know is that nature can heal, and there isn't a bad day that taking a walk-in nature can't fix.

Every person on this earth will benefit from spending time outside in nature. Your backyard will do fine. This is very necessary for empaths. Nothing works as well as nature to recharge and balance yourself instantly. It will be even better if you can walk barefoot.

- Regular Meditation

Empaths need to keep negative feelings and thoughts from staying in your mind. To help you do this, you need to meditate regularly. Meditation has proven to be the best protection tool.

Meditation helps you watch your thoughts, so negative ones can't enter your mind. It can also teach you to quiet your mind completely.

If a feeling or thought happens during the day, you need to ask yourself one question: "Is this my thought?" The majority of the time, it won't be your thought, and you have picked it up from another person.

- Time Management

This might seem like a mental tool rather than a protection tool, but truthfully, it's both. This happens because of empaths, like helping other people. It might be hard for you to tell others "no." This might cause you to lose a lot of time during your day. You have to learn ways to manage your time and say "no" to people's requests and projects. This is your best remedy.

You have to know what things drain your energy and learn to stay away from them. You have to learn how to manage your time so you can make sure you replenish your energy by getting out in nature and meditating.

- Love Yourself

You are precious. You have to remember this. Your daily mantra should be something like: “I am capable of being strong and vulnerable. I will embrace my sensitivities.”

You need to have regular alone time. You can create a shield of light and place it around yourself and make sure you have your crystals with you. When you are around other humans, you are going to be influenced by their vibrations. This might not be a big problem most of the time. If you don’t ever have time to be present with your vibrations, you might become an empath that is completely frazzled.

- Strong Intuition

You need to make your intuition stronger. Trust it to help you choose the right people to have in your circle. You have to keep energy vampires away at all costs. Your intuition will let you know if your energy decreases or increases when you are around certain people. You need to pay attention to this information. Try to stay around people who will increase your energy. Remember to get those boundaries set with the people who constantly drain your energy.

- Fresh Flowers

This one goes along with spending time in nature. Bringing flowers into your indoor space will give you an instant flow of refreshing energy. Flowers work on the same level as emotions, so they help reboot and repair. This is very important for empaths.

- Breathe

Do as much mindful breathing as you can throughout the day. Breathe out all the stress and negative energy, breathe in power and clarity. Your breath is your best friend. In order to be a warrior, you have to keep breathing out all the stress and negative energy during the day. This will keep stress from accumulating in your body.

Any type of deep breathing will recharge you very well. Old feelings could get clogged in your energetic field and body. Deep breathing could help dislodge these feelings and get rid of them. Breathing can flood you with cleansing energy and freshness, while at the same time, you will be receiving healing wisdom and divine information that gets encoded in the very air we breathe.

- Heart Meditation

When at all possible, do a three-minute heart meditation during your day to keep your heart energy centered and to keep the fear at bay. This meditation will work wonders to bring you back into your power once you begin to feel sensory overload. The heart meditation will make you stronger and puts you in charge of your emotions.

- Gratitude

Begin every day with an affirmation of gratitude rather than focusing on everything you need to do. Being grateful will increase your positive energy and will keep you at the moment instead of wasting your energy worrying about your future.

- Salt Baths

A couple of handfuls of either sea salt of Epsom salt dissolved in some warm water is the best thing you can do to clear and recharge your energy. Try to soak for 30 minutes and light some candles. Bless the water before you submerge yourself. Make sure you have drinking water and give that a blessing, too. You could point your palms toward the water and say something like: "Divine Presence, thank you for filling this water with vibrations of love, purification, and healing."

- Laugh Until You Cry

If you don't have a book, YouTube clip, cartoon, or movie that will make you laugh until you cry, you have to find one as soon as possible. If you have a family member or friend that regularly makes you laugh, you could always ask them to hit you up with a joke or two to make you laugh. Hard laughing can turn pain into a joy that flows (tears). It breaks down all the unhealthy defenses that you have built up as a strategy to help you survive, so you can connect with the world and nourish yourself.

- Drink and Eat Green Things

A healthy heart chakra will vibrate at the frequency of an emerald. Drinking beverages and eating foods that are full of chlorophyll like a green juice or green vegetables will bring this vibration into your heart to recharge it with the right amount of energy that you need. Green foods like avocados and kiwis are great, too. This stuff is great for you.

Remember that you have to clear your energy daily. If you can take care of your energy, you will find that being an empath turns into a superpower instead of a challenge.

Strengthening Your Abilities

Being an empath, you have the ability to connect with your higher self and get information that exceeds your physical senses. The most crucial part is the ability to hang on to an image for a long time.

Most empaths won't be able to hold onto this information so you can understand what you have received. The main thing to do is meditation. The best thing about meditation is it creates a great opportunity for you to connect to the Universe and the energy Source by using conscious intentions. The knowledge that passes through the cord that connects you to the Universe could feed your soul, but we normally can't hold it long enough to understand it in its fullness.

In most cases, you will get small visions or some mixed visions that you will have to put a lot of effort into to put them together to get the information out of them. At other times, you could get some strange sensations, feelings, or emotions, but you can't understand how they got to you and how they are connected. You might hear something very quickly, but it was too short to get anything from it. You could access some higher knowledge, but it was so light and fleeting that you won't be able to know if it was you or it came from the other realm.

When you are able to keep other people's energy away, the next step is to expand your intuition and increase your attention span. Each empath is different, and we all have our own way of dealing with things. A great way to help train your brain into keeping your visions for longer periods of time is to create mental images and see how long you can keep it there.

This might seem like something for newcomers but holding your sensory focus for several minutes takes a lot of effort. Our mind loves changing and will hop from one topic to the next without allowing you to decide if you want to. Our ego is always looking for ways to stay in power and control the situation. We've had the goal to keep that part separate from us.

For you to be able to develop your psychic abilities, hold a mental picture of any object for no less than 15 seconds. You can change the number of seconds based on how well you currently focus and work your way on up during your mindful breathing daily.

Don't just increase the number of seconds you can hold the image. You have to be able to see it with as much aliveness and clarity as you possibly can. It isn't about quantity here; it is about quality.

There's no need to worry, while you are making an effort in creating your mental image as vivid and clear as possible, you won't even be aware that you are doing it for longer time periods.

During the first week or so, just try to imagine a simple spiral or colored dot. It can be any color you choose. If it is a color you resonate with, it will work a lot better. Once you begin making progress, you make it more fun by creating more details to put in the picture.

It's important that you begin with a simple object when you are starting to improve your abilities. After about a week or so of consistent practice, it will amaze you at how well you have gotten in keeping your focus. By the time you realize it, you will have a vivid, clear picture that has come from your spirit guides or our higher self, whichever you connect with more. All those vague, blurry pictures will get replaced with lively, colorful pictures.

Once you have taught yourself to hold onto visions for a long time, being able to extract more information will get better, too. The secret is working at it constantly.

Another great way to improve your abilities is to keep emotion in your heart. This nurtures your intuition and will keep a positive emotion in your heart. Positive emotions could be anything from a deep fondness to a wonderful affection that feels like it can absorb the entire body, mind, and heart.

This emotion could feel like a living, breathing organism. It might feel light and loving.

Try to place this feeling inside yourself and spread it to every area of your body. You need to hold it there for as long as possible and silence your mind to let your intuition to present itself.

This is great if you want to deepen your intuition through emotions or visualizations. Each second you spend with a positive emotion inside your heart, space will count. I won't improve your ability to understand complex information that is coming through, but it will feed your soul for a long time.

This ability will serve you well. If you encounter negative people that look at you as prey, you won't have any problems connecting your intuitive side to your heart. This will recreate the emotion you've been practicing and will create an invisible barrier that negative people can't get through.

The power to be able to immediately tap into this loving and safe environment at any time is priceless. This is what being emotionally focused will give to you. You can refine this skill by implementing or amplifying minor details to your object by increasing its beauty or the emotions you are feeling.

You can bring any emotion into your heart space. You can bring in affection, appreciation, and kindness. You can arrange these emotions on top of each other like emotional coats and see how many you can hold at one time.

Keeping many emotions in your heart space at one time will get you in tune with your multi-dimensional consciousness. Our brains are used to interpreting things linearly. Creating a multi-dimensional consciousness will give you the ability to work on several things at once.

Having a multi-dimensional consciousness will refine your ability to keep feelings in your physical space and to hold onto many ideas at one time. This will help you advance your clairvoyance. It isn't just good for your clairvoyance but will help other spiritual gifts.

Clairaudience is an ability to you can enhance by bringing your attention to voices and sounds from your surroundings. Using the solfeggio frequencies can start you on your clairaudience journey. These frequencies resonate deeply in our nature, so we are able to hold focus for longer.

Claircognizance is the sense of knowing things. The key to developing this ability is to focus on the present moment for as long as you can. You can enhance this ability by trying to sustain a still mind without letting any thoughts come into it. Fill your mind with a picture of a white, pure crystal. By doing this, you are making room for claircognizance to come in a while, asking your consciousness to move aside.

Each person has natural spiritual gifts, and for many, these have been dormant for years. They have become paralyzed due to no activity. In order to allow claircognizance to come through, place your focus on quieting your mind. Try to focus on clarity and dissolving your ego, and you will get a chance to touch on something that will exceed all physical senses.

It is more about surrendering your conscious mind and letting to unconscious move forward. Once you become aware that you are receiving higher information from the outer realm, you will know that you can handle all the information it gives to you.

This higher self will be able to help you decipher the messages that you get and the ways you can use them with your current situation. Don't worry about losing the connection you made with your higher self. Once you make contact, it will be easy to reach it again.

If you are having problems understand the information you get, it is probably because you haven't been paying attention to the spiritual realm, and you have a lot of unused abilities.

With some practice, you will be able to increase your capacity to keep your focus and be able to channel any knowledge that the cosmos is willing to give you. Your focus is what creates the link between you and the psychic realm. It is very important to practice as much as you can to hone your skills to be able to tune into what your higher self and spirit guides are trying to tell you. It is hard for them to connect with you if you are there for a moment, and then you aren't. They can't communicate with you this way.

You have to develop your psychic focus so you can stay longer in the spirit realm so your higher self and spirit guides will be able to help you solve your problems and help you get things done, be on time, and meet your deadlines. They will increase your vibration and make you wiser so you can make the world better.

You need to practice a couple of times daily, and as you get better, you will realize that you have received information, but you couldn't see the difference between it and your daily thoughts, or your ego took all the credit.

Your emotional mind and body will get more stable, and the information coming from your spirit guides will increase when your empath abilities get stronger.

The journey of an empath is a lifetime adventure. Being a sensitive person, there will always be things to be grateful for. You will experience exquisite joy and passion. You will be able to see the big picture on levels that are so much deeper. You will be in tune with all the energy, poetry, and beauty in your life. All your compassion will give you the ability to help others in ways you never imagined. You are never coldhearted, shut off, or callous. These sensitivities let you be vulnerable, caring, and always aware of just being.

You will see your own relationships and life improve when you embrace your Warrior Empath. Every time you make progress by centering yourself during the chaos, asserting your needs, or listening to your intuition, you need to celebrate. When you stop denying your feeling just to make others comfortable, celebrate. When you learn to see yourself as beautiful without second-guessing yourself or conflicting feelings, celebrate. Learn to be grateful for any progress you've made. Cherish these baby steps as they are golden. If you backslide, don't worry about it. Everyone does. Whatever happens, be compassionate with yourself.

Conclusion

Thank you for making it through to the end of *Empath Healing*, let's hope it was informative and able to provide you with all of the tools you need to achieve your goals whatever they may be.

It is time for you to start taking care of yourself and allow your gift to flourish. Empaths are a special part of society, even though society does not understand them. We are the people that others turn to in their time of need because they know we can help. Yes, it can be scary. As empaths, we are more vulnerable to people like narcissists and energy vampires. But with the information in this book, you have a good basis on how to avoid them.

If you are like me, and most other empaths, you probably already have some wounds to heal from. But you can learn from me and others on the best ways to overcome these wounds. We've covered quite a few things that you can do to help improve and heal yourself. The most important thing is to learn that you can put yourself first. As empaths, we feel deeply for others, but that doesn't mean we have to put their needs before our own. If we continue to give and give and give, we won't have anything left to give, and we definitely won't be able to help others and ourselves.

You now have a very good understanding of what you are and the abilities you have. You know that you aren't some overly sensitive person, but instead, an empath who feels things more deeply than others. You can spot energy vampires and narcissists, and you will no longer allow them to control you. You also should have a good understanding of how to listen to your body and tune into your emotions. This is important so that you don't get lost in the emotions and energy of others.

You are here to make the world a better place, but on your terms and not to your own detriment. You are number one in life, and by taking care of yourself, you can help to heal the world and make it a better place. You are not a burden, no matter what you were told growing up. You are a gift, and you have the right to let that gift shine. Make sure, if you have children, that you give them the space to grow and flourish if they are also blessed with the gift of empathy.

Make sure that you work through chapters five until chapter nine. They are going to help you tremendously. If you are in immediate need of healing, make sure you refer to chapter eight. I know you can be the powerful empath that you are meant to be. You are a strong and amazing person, and you are meant to do wonderful things.

Lastly, if you are interested in learning more about healing other people, make sure you check out my other books and empathy and narcissistic abuse.

Finally, if you found this book useful in any way, a review on Amazon is always appreciated!

Reviews are crucial for a book to thrive on Amazon; otherwise the book will simply die away. Hence our survival as authors and publishers heavily depend on them. So, if you found this book useful in any way, I would love to see a review from you with a simple feedback on what you liked, what can be improved and, of course, please feel free to share your experience with your fellow readers.

Thank you so much reading to the end of this book and I wish you good luck on your endeavors!

CPSIA information can be obtained
at www.ICGtesting.com
Printed in the USA
BVHW061015230120
570300BV00013B/1160